HOW WHALE/WELL CAN YOU SPELL?

MARIA T. HOWARD

iUniverse, Inc.
Bloomington

HOW WHALE/WELL CAN YOU SPELL?

iUniverse books may be ordered through booksellers or by contacting:

iUniverse
1663 Liberty Drive
Bloomington, IN 47403
www.iuniverse.com
1-800-Authors (1-800-288-4677)

Because of the dynamic nature of the Internet, any Web addresses or links contained in this book may have changed since publication and may no longer be valid.

ISBN: 978-1-4502-5229-4 (sc)
ISBN: 978-1-4502-5230-0 (ebk)

Printed in the United States of America

iUniverse rev. date: 1/17/2011

ACKNOWLEDGEMENT

I wish to express my gratitude to my friends, family, and educators for their encouragement throughout my project. Thank you for provided me with invaluable moral support and guidance. You encouraged me to hang in there and not quit.

A special thanks to iUniverse staff for compiling my project and for constant support and editorial assistance. Thanks for your hard work and dedication.

1.	ttuch	tuoch	tuosh	touch
2.	frenid	freind	friend	frieend
3.	paper	papur	peper	papper
4.	medicane	medicine	madacine	medicane
5.	soaial	sociel	soscial	social
6.	desserve	diserve	deserve	deserfe
7.	bizarre	beizerre	bezzare	bezare
8.	prempt	promapt	prompt	praumpt
9.	beatiful	beautiful	biautifol	beautefull
10.	bisiness	busaness	business	buseness
11.	secret	sacreat	seecret	secriete
12.	plasktick	plestick	plastic	peastic
13.	interest	nterast	enterest	intarast
14.	travvel	travel	trevel	travul
15.	tueetion	tuishion	tuiition	tuition
16.	terrific	terriffice	terrificc	terifficc
17.	acedemey	academy	accedamey	acedemy
18.	redy	reddy	ready	readi
19.	gorgeus	gorgous	gorgeous	gurgeous

20.	happer	hapier	happier	happoir
21.	played	plaiyed	playedd	plaeyed
22.	puch	push	osch	pushh
23.	enternetional	international	intereational	nterneationeel
24.	decision	decssion	dcision	desion
25.	mension	menton	mintion	mention
26.	acceptance	aceptence	ackceptance	aceptense
27.	recignion	recontion	recognesion	recognition
28.	familiar	fimialiar	famelier	familier
29.	calandur	calendar	celendar	culendar
30.	gradasion	graduation	graduetion	graduasion
31.	accusation	accusetion	acusation	akusation
32.	meeningful	meaningfull	meaningful	meangful
33.	perfect	perfuct	purfect	pirfact
34.	bcause	becose	becuase	because
35.	vecation	vacasion	vecetion	vacation
36.	sensible	sensble	sencible	sensbel
37.	publicasion	publication	pubication	publicaktion
38.	fourtunate	fortunate	fortonuate	fortunete

39.	adaptation	adeption	adation	adaptsion
40.	happiness	hapiness	happeness	happinass
41.	raciprocate	reciprocate	recipocate	receprocate
42.	chamecial	kemical	chemecal	chemical
43.	resentely	recently	recenty	recentlee
44.	finally	finaly	finallee	finaly
45.	ilaborate	elabourete	elaberete	elaborate
46.	nursery	nersury	nersurey	nursary
47.	changable	shangeable	changeable	chajeable
48.	sherish	chareish	cherich	cherish
49.	hamrliss	harmliss	hurmless	harmless
50.	furher	furthar	furter	further
51.	collaboration	colaboration	colleboration	cullaboration
52.	relationship	relashioiship	reletionship	relationshap
53.	adrress	address	addres	addrasses
54.	dececsion	decasion	decition	decision
55.	saparation	seperation	seperesion	separation
56.	unlimited	ulimited	unlemeted	onlimitad
57.	dependable	dipendeble	dependible	depandable

58.	curtainly	certainly	cuertainly	surtianlie
59.	relity	realety	reality	releity
60.	indepandant	idependent	indapendent	independent
61.	defferince	diference	diffarence	difference
62.	popelar	pupolar	popular	poplar
63.	imotion	emotion	emosion	emution
64.	segneficant	sigficant	significant	signeficant
65.	proportion	proption	propertion	preportion
66.	dedicated	dicated	dedecated	dediceted
67.	uiversity	university	uneversity	universety
68.	desperate	despirite	desperaete	deperate
69.	idantify	idintify	identify	identafy
70.	between	btwen	betweeen	betweenn
71.	fluid	flueed	fliud	fluied
72.	concluseve	conclusive	cunclusive	conclosive
73.	drametically	dramatically	dramaticelly	drematecally
74.	conclusion	conclution	concluson	cunclusion
75.	techniqes	technequeas	technique	teckniques
76.	relex	ralax	releax	relax

77.	huamster	hamstor	hemster	hamster
78.	company	kompany	compenie	compeny
79.	introduction	entroduction	introdection	intruducton
80.	highway	hghway	hiway	highwey
81.	tention	tension	tansion	tenson
82.	shinese	chinese	chineese	chieneese
83.	relfection	reflaction	reflection	refliction
84.	risponsibility	responsebelety	respunsbility	responsibility
85.	continuasion	conteneuation	contenuation	continuation
86.	sweter	sweator	sweatur	sweater
87.	heater	heter	heator	heatur
88.	temperature	temperator	tempurature	tamperature
89.	proveke	provoke	proveke	prevolke
90.	fraustration	frustration	frostration	frustrsion
91.	cantinue	contine	continue	cuntenue
92.	almanac	almenec	almanec	almenack
93.	sircumstance	surcumstance	circumstance	curcumstance
94.	estimate	etimate	estemete	stimate
95.	dimaned	demended	demanded	demandad

96.	genetic	ginetic	ginetick	genatic
97.	adicted	addicted	addected	addicked
98.	apliance	appliance	applince	applianse
99.	racognietion	racognitiion	recugnition	recognition
100.	puncture	poncture	punture	puncshure
101.	strite	straight	stiaight	saight
102.	development	davelopmant	devalopment	develupmint
103.	enrolment	enrallmant	enrollment	enrullment
104.	dramtic	draumetick	dramatic	draumatic
105.	elemenation	eliminasion	elimenition	elimination
106.	height	hieght	heigt	highte
107.	mountain	montaen	mounten	mountin
108.	anvalope	envelope	enveloupe	nvelope
109.	londry	laundrie	laundry	landry
110.	lether	leathir	leathur	leather
111.	jacket	jaket	jackat	jaket
112.	cheeese	cheese	cheessee	cheesse
113.	discant	discount	discoun	descount
114.	detirgint	detergint	ditergent	detergent

115.	produc	prduce	producce	produce
116.	galon	gallun	galllan	gallon
117.	quality	qualetie	qualityie	qualety
118.	itinerary	itenerary	itinarary	itineriy
119.	encyclaoupedia	encyclopedia	ncylopadia	encyclopideia
120.	problem	preblem	praublem	problim
121.	souphistication	sophistication	sufeistication	sophesticaiton
122.	cliam	claim	klaim	claime
123.	remourse	remorsse	remorse	remorce
124.	difendant	defendint	defendant	defiendant
125.	nieghour	neighbour	neigbor	neighbor
126.	braught	brough	brught	brought
127.	argument	argament	argumint	argumant
128.	scoooter	scooter	sooter	sckooter
129.	refreigerator	refrigerator	rifregetaor	refregartaor
130.	intervine	intiervene	intervene	interviene
131.	intermission	intermision	inturmistion	intermession
132.	tomorow	tomorrow	tommorrow	tmorrow
133.	magnefecent	magnificent	magnifiscent	magnificant

134.	fascinated	fascineted	facinated	fasceneted
135.	pulitics	poletics	politicks	politics
136.	socialy	socielly	sociely	socially
137.	profession	prufession	profesion	profassion
138.	language	languge	lenguage	lanuage
139.	esentials	essenteal	essential	esenteils
140.	notice	nutise	noticce	notece
141.	estemete	estimete	estimate	estemate
142.	economie	economy	ecunumy	ecunomy
143.	dumbbill	dumbball	dumbell	dumbbell
144.	security	cecurity	securety	sekurity
145.	suplaier	supplair	sopplier	supplier
146.	truble	trouble	trubole	troubel
147.	shure	chur	sure	sare
148.	rough	ruff	rougf	rughf
149.	criminal	cremeinal	cremenal	criminel
150.	shool	school	schol	schoool
151.	finenacial	finenencial	financial	fiannceial
152.	reskeu	rescue	recue	riscue

153.	federal	fidieral	faderal	federaul
154.	endustry	indostry	ndustry	industry
155.	execautive	executive	xecutive	exacative
156.	recisison	recesstion	recession	ricession
157.	though	thaugh	tthough	thouggh
158.	spiral	sperial	pirel	spiraul
159.	suppart	support	suport	suppart
160.	minimize	minimizze	mennimize	minimice
161.	choreographer	cherografer	choregraper	charepgrefer
162.	comercial	commercial	commerseial	commerceial
163.	xcluasive	exclosive	exclusive	xclusive
164.	document	documint	documant	ducoment
165.	oreignal	origeneal	original	uoriginal
166.	restaurint	ristaruent	restuarant	restaurant
167.	confuse	cunfuse	konfuse	confusse
168.	transpher	transfer	traunsfer	transfur
169.	around	arund	arround	araund
170.	conection	connection	cunnection	connaction
171.	exceteid	exceited	excitaed	excited

172.	empress	impress	impres	impriss
173.	allawence	alowence	allowance	allowence
174.	reelize	relize	realize	realise
175.	humour	humor	houmor	humur
176.	auful	awfull	awful	ouful
177.	clasified	classified	classeified	clessified
178.	estimate	estiemate	estimete	estemiate
179.	resposible	responsible	responsibel	risponsible
180.	disigner	desiger	designir	designer
181.	apointment	appointmint	appoiment	appointment
182.	emergiency	emergancy	emirgency	emergency
183.	liquidation	liquediation	liquidetion	liquiasion
184.	computur	computer	computir	computur
185.	digitel	digitul	degital	digital
186.	anxious	anxouis	anxius	anxouis
187.	imediately	immediataly	immediately	immidiately
188.	century	sentury	centery	centiry
189.	spaciael	special	speciall	spescial
190.	fantastic	fantiastick	fantastec	fantestic

191.	majastick	majestic	majestick	mejestic
192.	kollection	collaction	collection	colection
193.	personalety	personality	pursonality	persunalitly
194.	cumfortable	comfourtable	comforteble	comfortable
195.	direction	derection	dirction	direcktion
196.	faous	famous	famuos	femaous
197.	leisure	liesure	leishure	leisare
198.	critick	cretick	critic	critec
199.	dicade	dacade	decade	decde
200.	netion	netional	nationel	national
201.	xpert	expert	expurt	expiert
202.	represent	represant	raprasent	reprecent
203.	weird	wierd	wird	weerd
204.	definetion	definition	difinition	difenition
205.	rediculous	rideculous	redecluos	ridiculous
206.	satifesfection	satisfication	satisfection	satisfaction
207.	setuation	situation	sitoution	situetion
208.	multiypurposse	moltiperpose	multipurpose	multyperpose
209.	imagenetion	emagination	imagination	imagnation

210.	hospital	hospetial	hospetal	huspital
211.	atomobile	atomobille	autamobile	automobile
212.	American	Americen	Aerican	Amarican
213.	spelling	speling	spelleang	spellang
214.	oportunaty	opportunity	opportaniety	opportanity
215.	activeity	activity	actevety	activitee
216.	enegy	aner	anergy	energy
217.	exarcsise	exercase	exercise	exercse
218.	inspired	enspired	inspared	enspiared
219.	hurricane	hurryicene	huricene	huricane
220.	baerd	beard	bired	beered
221.	numeric	numerick	mumaric	numarick
222.	feetures	feeataures	features	fiteaures
223.	numorous	numorus	nomorous	numerous
224.	process	procass	praucess	procss
225.	pament	payment	paymant	paymint
226.	transetion	transition	transision	trensition
227.	receipt	recieipt	recipt	recept
228.	dimond	diamend	diamond	dymond

229.	childen	childran	children	childrin
230.	storaje	storage	sturage	sturege
231.	luxury	luxaury	luxurary	luxuree
232.	furniture	furnitshure	firniture	firnature
233.	uion	union	unoin	nion
234.	Holywood	Hollywood	Hollywod	Hollywould
235.	grociry	growcery	grocery	graucery
236.	bautel	botel	bottlle	bottle
237.	valey	vallay	vallie	valley
238.	avenew	avaneu	avenue	aveknew
239.	climate	climete	climaite	klimate
240.	pioneer	pionear	pionnear	poineir
241.	lemonaide	lemonade	limonade	lamonade
242.	national	netional	nashional	natonal
243.	pledje	pledge	pladge	plege
244.	problim	prublem	problem	poblem
245.	senseitonal	sensetional	censational	sensational
246.	carnation	karnetion	carnetion	karnation
247.	daisas	daisies	dases	daseis

248.	jungle	jungel	jangle	jongle
249.	background	bacground	backgound	bacgrund
250.	summary	sumary	summery	sumerry
251.	summarise	sumarize	sumaricise	summarize
252.	daffodil	dafodil	dafodel	daffodel
253.	iis	iris	iras	eyeris
254.	maregold	marigald	marigold	marygold
255.	orchid	orchad	ourchid	orcheed
256.	tulop	toolip	tulap	tulip
257.	surgary	surgery	sirgery	surgiry
258.	disturb	dasturb	desturb	diturb
259.	arogent	arrogant	arogant	arragant
260.	anoy	anay	annoye	annoy
261.	combative	combetive	kombative	cumbative
262.	konfuse	confuse	conphuse	confus
263.	candemn	condem	condemn	kondemn
264.	massive	messive	massevie	messeve
265.	mineatare	miniature	minature	minitare
266.	imense	immanse	immense	immence

267.	Germeny	Jermany	Garmane	Germany
268.	France	Franse	Frence	Frannce
269.	Maxico	Mexico	Meico	Mexeco
270.	Englend	Englind	England	Angland
271.	Chena	Chine	Schina	China
272.	Doberman	Dobermein	Doburman	Dobirman
273.	Poodel	Poodle	Poddle	Poodkle
274.	Boxar	Boxier	Boxer	Boxir
275.	Rottwieler	Rottweilar	Rottweiler	Rottwielir
276.	Colie	Collie	Kollie	Cullie
277.	valuabel	valuible	valuble	valuable
278.	inturmedeate	inturmediate	intermidiate	intermediate
279.	settler	sattler	sittler	settlir
280.	euqeliety	equallity	equality	equeleity
281.	noticeabel	noticeble	noticeable	noticeeble
282.	ofendar	offendir	offinder	offender
283.	Pelgrem	Pilgrim	Pillgrim	Pilgream
284.	exploarer	explorir	explorer	explarer
285.	scarcity	scarecity	scerceity	scarcety

286.	Thenksgiving	Thansgevign	Thanksgeveing	Thanksgiving
287.	lendford	landform	landfourm	laendform
288.	seeson	seasun	season	seesun
289.	timeline	tameline	tymeline	timline
290.	rivur	rever	river	rivar
291.	pennsula	pinensula	peninsula	penensila
292.	menester	minster	ministur	minister
293.	paradde	perede	parad	parade
294.	freedom	freedum	friedom	fradom
295.	standerd	standard	stendard	stardurd
296.	coureje	couoreage	courage	corage
297.	downlad	download	douwnload	downlod
298.	backward	bacward	backword	beckward
299.	inpsired	enspired	inspared	inspired
300.	houspital	hospetal	hospital	huspital
301.	grammar	grammur	gremar	gramar
302.	vocabulery	vacublary	vocabulary	vucabulary
303.	screem	scream	sckream	screem
304.	trenslation	transleshion	transelation	translation

305.	disketes	deskettes	diskettes	diskittes
306.	dynamie	dynaemite	dianamie	dynamite
307.	nheritance	enheritence	inharatance	inheritance
308.	attachment	atachmint	attachmant	atachmint
309.	unswer	ansir	anwer	answer
310.	presencce	precence	precsence	presence
311.	mountains	mountens	mountians	montains
312.	eneiy	eniemy	enamy	enemy
313.	tribelation	tribulation	tribolation	treebulation
314.	Rusha	Russia	Rusia	Rusia
315.	generosiety	ganarosity	gienerosity	generosity
316.	imetation	emetation	imitation	imitatin
317.	vegetables	vegetabels	vegitables	vegetibles
318.	convence	convinse	convice	convince
319.	exerise	exercise	exarcise	exersice
320.	measure	meashure	meshure	measre
321.	unyform	uniform	uform	unyiform
322.	strength	strangth	strenght	strangth
323.	against	agains	aginst	agenst

324.	eritege	heritage	haritage	heriteje
325.	continue	cuntienue	continew	cuntenew
326.	seetizen	sitizen	citezen	citizen
327.	rocket	rockat	rucket	roket
328.	paece	peacee	peece	peace
329.	tetile	textile	taxtile	textale
330.	employer	empluyer	amployer	epluyer
331.	tranfir	tranfer	transfer	trasfur
332.	youtah	uta	uttah	Utah
333.	temporary	temporay	tempurary	tamporary
334.	toughh	tough	tuff	touhg
335.	reaktion	reaction	rection	reackshon
336.	precious	precous	precoius	preshons
337.	defesnes	defense	defence	definse
338.	acquainteed	aquainted	acquainted	ackquainted
339.	kowladge	knowleage	knowladge	knowledge
340.	apologee	apoulogy	apolougy	apology
341.	scrutinize	scrutinise	skrutinize	screwtinize
342.	detective	detectave	ditective	detecktive

343.	vacashion	vacation	vecation	vecashion
344.	terminal	turminel	termenel	turminal
345.	antecepate	anticipaete	anticipate	andicipate
346.	facktory	factoury	factory	factury
347.	together	togethur	tgether	togethir
348.	gentlemen	gentlaman	gentlimen	gantleman
349.	llcation	location	locetion	locaton
350.	vicktory	victury	victury	victory
351.	fruit	fruite	friute	froot
352.	employement	employment	emplaymint	empoyment
353.	headacke	hadache	headache	haedhache
354.	siegnature	signaturre	signature	segnature
355.	guarentee	guerenatee	guarentee	guarantee
356.	monster	monstire	munster	monstur
357.	wealth	wealh	welth	wealh
358.	grupe	group	gruip	groop
359.	dolar	dollar	dullar	dolllar
360.	viseble	visibel	visible	vasible
361.	forbiden	fourbidden	forbidden	forbiden

362.	emit	emiitt	emati	emat
363.	devastaat	divastated	davasted	devastated
364.	daugthir	daughtur	daughtier	daughter
365.	facilety	facelity	faciliety	facility
366.	abeliety	abilitee	abelity	ability
367.	incredble	incredible	incredibel	incridible
368.	famous	famouse	famos	femaous
369.	destruction	destructon	distruction	destriction
370.	functon	function	fanction	funcktion
371.	blezzard	blizzeard	blezzard	blizzard
372.	Philadelphia	Philadelphea	Phaladelphia	Philadilphia
373.	Georgia	Georgea	Geargiia	Georgea
374.	parmit	permit	permitt	purmit
375.	convertible	cunvertibel	cunvertible	convirtible
376.	Califournia	Calefornia	Califurnia	California
377.	basicelly	basically	besicelly	basicaly
378.	peculair	paculiar	peculiar	pekuliar
379.	purchasse	purchase	perchuase	purchese
380.	strenje	stranje	strenge	strange

381.	surround	suround	surrand	surruond
382.	beauty	bauety	beauety	beuty
383.	promuton	promoshon	promoution	promotion
384.	scisor	scissor	scissir	scissur
385.	million	milloin	meelion	milon
386.	Commissioner	Cummissioer	Comissioner	Comissioner
387.	lightning	lightneng	lightening	leghtning
388.	confuson	cunfusion	conphusion	confusion
389.	establish	establesh	estiblash	estableash
390.	Connecticat	Connecticut	Conecticut	Connacticut
391.	investigation	investagetion	invistigation	investegaton
392.	aparetment	apartment	apartmint	apartement
393.	identafy	idientify	identifay	identify
394.	energy	enrgy	enargy	enirgy
395.	narate	nuarrate	narrate	narratte
396.	narrative	nerrative	narretive	narative
397.	narratir	nerretaor	nerrator	narrator
398.	purtain	pertain	pirtane	purtane
399.	prudain	prudente	pruddaint	prudent

400.	multitode	multiude	multitude	multetude
401.	calamity	calemeity	calameity	calamety
402.	transgression	transgrassion	trengrassion	transgrasion
403.	separetes	separates	separatas	separetes
404.	reveall	reveal	revael	reveall
405.	subscripton	subscription	sabscription	subscreption
406.	instution	instructoin	nstruction	instruction
407.	persuade	persade	pursaudaes	persuadis
408.	continue	continu	contenue	contenui
409.	proportoin	proportion	propertion	propurtion
410.	propertee	pruperty	property	propirty
411.	emution	emation	emotoin	emotion
412.	ourdinary	ordenary	ordinery	ordinary
413.	respect	respact	rispect	respeck
414.	jewelree	jewelry	jawelry	jewwelry
415.	warenty	warrenty	warrenaty	warranty
416.	kcountry	counntry	contry	country
417.	photagrph	photograph	fotograph	photogreaph
418.	veiwer	vieweer	viewer	vewier

419.	suddenly	suddantly	suddently	suddanlee
420.	charetiy	charity	charety	chareety
421.	dissolve	disolve	dissolv	dessolve
422.	astoneishment	astanishment	astonishment	astonishmint
423.	creatur	creeture	creature	kreature
424.	fugitive	fugetive	fugetiv	fagitive
425.	manufactur	menufactue	mannufacture	manufacture
426.	approprete	appropreite	appropriat	appropriate
427.	authority	athority	autority	autharirty
428.	cuntinualy	continually	continualy	cuntinualy
429.	konsederation	consideration	consederation	considireation
430.	compure	copare	compare	cumpare
431.	wharehouse	werehouse	warehouse	warehase
432.	station	stetion	statoin	stetion
433.	contemplate	contemplat	cuntimplate	comtimplate
434.	discuss	descuss	discass	discusss
435.	lobstir	lobster	lubster	lobstar
436.	efort	effort	effoart	effart
437.	air	aur	aer	aire

438.	attorney	atoreney	atterney	atorney
439.	numirator	newmerator	numeratir	numerator
440.	milleonaire	milionaire	millionaire	milloinaire
441.	science	sciennce	cience	sience
442.	dancer	dancir	dencier	dancur
443.	wisdum	wiesdum	wisdom	wesdum
444.	hafe	halkf	hafl	half
445.	dangeros	dangerouss	dengaraous	dangerous
446.	eveang	evenang	eveing	evening
447.	preposetion	preposation	preposition	proposation
448.	characker	character	cheractor	charackter
449.	presenter	presanter	presinter	presintur
450.	denominair	denouminator	denominator	denominetor
451.	fourht	faruth	fourth	fourrth
452.	third	thrdi	thard	thurd
453.	compromise	cumprumece	comprimice	comprumise
454.	horoscpae	horoskope	horoscoupe	horoscope
455.	horezontal	horizental	horizontal	hourizontal
456.	several	severil	savaral	seviral

457.	recuncileation	reconciliation	reconseliation	reconcilation
458.	necesity	necessity	necesiety	necessatiy
459.	roomette	roommete	rommate	roommate
460.	inkome	incomme	income	incume
461.	expanse	expence	expens	expense
462.	increase	increese	encrease	increas
463.	labor	lebur	labir	labur
464.	rcourse	resaurce	resource	resarce
465.	shuld	should	shuld	chould
466.	hopfully	hopefuly	hopefally	hopefully
467.	furthir	furthor	furtor	further
468.	officeul	oficeil	officiel	official
469.	civilian	civileian	sivilian	ceivlian
470.	earthquake	erthquake	earthqake	earthquek
471.	petient	patient	pateint	petiant
472.	Cheroke	Cherokee	Cherakee	Cherockee
473.	garaje	garage	geraje	garae
474.	enaguration	inajuration	inauguration	inaugoretion
475.	triplet	treeplet	triple	triplat

476.	refusal	refusel	rephusal	riefusal
477.	procrastenete	procrastinate	procrastinete	prokrastinate
478 .	compasion	compason	compssion	compassion
479.	traffic	traffick	treffick	trafic
480.	problum	probleim	problem	prublem
481.	meteoroulogest	metiorologest	metrologiest	meteorologist
482.	ahed	ahaed	ahead	ahhead
483.	bellbord	billbord	billboard	bellboard
484.	toothbrush	tooothbrrush	tothbrash	tothbruch
485.	seefood	seafod	cfood	seafood
486	inserance	ensurance	inurance	insurance
487.	urgent	urjent	urgint	ergent
488.	bridge	bridje	bredge	braidge
489.	amont	amount	amoant	amant
490.	depind	depend	dipend	depiend
491.	kitchan	ketchen	kitchen	kitchin
492.	cleanur	cleanir	cleanUr	cleaner
493.	customer	customir	costomer	custamer
494.	transmission	transmsion	transmession	tranmisson

495.	permision	permission	purmission	pirmisson
496.	freedom	freedam	friedom	frideeom
497.	therappy	therupy	tharapy	therapy
498.	reduction	reducsion	redaction	reducktion
499.	community	comunity	comminity	cammonity
500.	cornir	corner	cornur	cornor
501.	husband	hasbend	husbend	hosband
502.	theatir	teather	theater	theeter
503.	shoulldir	sholder	shuolder	shoulder
504.	whethaer	wether	whethir	whether
505.	material	meteriel	matereal	meteriel
506.	availabel	available	avoilable	availuble
507.	cunversetion	conversation	confersation	cunversaton
508.	exemple	xample	example	exempple
509.	Christmas	Christemes	Christmes	Chrastmas
510.	dekuration	deceration	decuration	decoration
511.	expienseive	expensavie	expansive	expensive
512.	natural	naturel	neturel	nateraul
513.	formula	formela	furmula	fourmala

514.	transciept	transcript	trenscript	transcrept
515.	leaguie	leegue	league	leajue
516.	leadership	leadershap	leeadership	laedership
517.	magazene	majaginze	magezine	magazine
518.	standurd	standerd	stendeard	standard
519.	acrusss	acruoss	acros	across
520.	navigate	navegete	navijage	nvigate
521.	plastick	plastic	plustic	plaustic
522.	literally	literelay	literelly	litirally
523.	freezir	freezer	frezer	freezur
524.	consimer	consumir	consumer	cunsumer
525.	producteive	prodactive	productive	prodactive
526.	therapiest	therapest	thaurepist	therapist
527.	graeter	graetur	greatir	greater
528.	counselor	counsalor	counselur	counsalir
529.	realtor	reator	realtier	realtiur
530.	anusement	amusement	amusameint	amusemant
531.	veterenery	veterinery	vaterenery	veterinary
532.	optican	upticein	optician	optetician

533.	kompany	cumpany	company	cumpeny
534.	pharmacy	farmacy	phuarmacy	pharmacie
535.	helth	haelth	halth	health
536.	mesage	messaje	messege	message
537.	restrant	restrint	restriant	restraint
538.	harvist	harveast	haurvest	harvest
539.	partner	partnur	parner	partnir
540.	anual	annual	anuel	annaull
541.	percentage	purcentage	pircinctage	percantage
542.	equiety	equity	equety	equaity
543.	divede	diviede	devide	divide
544.	multiply	multply	moltiply	multeply
545.	fraection	fraction	fractshion	frection
546.	luminous	luminos	lumenous	laminous
547.	kiten	citten	kitten	ketten
548.	condactor	conductor	cunductor	cunducter
549.	factery	factoury	factury	factory
550.	warning	waurning	warnening	warnning
551.	warehuse	warehouse	werehouse	warahuse

552.	afternun	afernoon	afturnoon	afternoon
553.	arund	araund	arround	around
554.	trumpet	trompit	trummpet	trumppet
555.	frantic	frentic	phrantic	frantec
556.	kendergerten	kindergarten	kindergurten	kindrgaten
557.	anemels	animels	animals	anemals
558.	riveiw	revew	raview	review
559.	burthday	berthday	barthday	birthday
560.	govermint	guverment	govirment	government
561.	literacy	lateracy	literasy	leterarcy
562.	dengerus	dangerous	danjgerous	dangerus
563.	enugh	enouph	enouf	enough
564.	geametry	geometry	geomatry	geomitry
565.	mddle	meddle	middel	middle
566.	anothar	anuther	another	anuthir
567.	basemint	bassement	basement	bassmint
568.	upstairs	upsteirs	upstares	ustairs
569.	picknick	peneck	picnic	pacnick
570.	cestle	castel	castle	kastle

571.	acedent	accidant	accident	ackident
572.	laugf	luagh	laugh	laph
573.	mattress	mattres	matriss	mattres
574.	karpet	curpet	carpat	carpet
575.	reson	reasin	reasun	reason
576.	tremble	tramble	treamble	trembel
577.	rchard	orchard	archard	orcherd
578.	heavy	hevy	heevy	haevy
579.	murning	marning	morning	mornang
580.	nature	neture	netshure	natjure
581.	already	allredy	alrdy	alraedy
582.	agen	agaiin	again	agein
583.	surprice	surprise	sirprise	surpraise
584.	piece	piese	piecce	peece
585.	wreitten	written	writtain	writtein
586.	onbuton	unbuton	unbuton	unbutton
587.	porcch	purch	porch	pourch
588.	elevator	elevaitor	elevatuor	elevetur
589.	escallatte	escalate	escelete	esclalaut

590.	aproch	approch	approach	appraoch
591.	official	offeciel	officeial	officel
592.	leder	laeder	leeder	leader
593.	ffective	effecteve	effective	effitive
594.	jrnal	journal	jornal	juornel
595.	applicaton	appliceation	applecetion	application
596.	Febraury	Februry	February	Februery
597.	collection	colletion	collaction	cullection
598.	Wednasday	Wednesday	Wednesdai	Wadnesday
599.	acadimy	ackademy	acadamy	academy
600.	Thirsday	Thuirsday	Thirsday	Thursday
601.	several	severul	severel	saveral
602.	symbal	symbol	symbel	simbal
603.	piano	paino	peenio	painoe
604.	curten	curtain	cirtain	kurtain
605.	cmpromise	cumpromese	compromise	compramese
606.	gaenius	genus	genius	gneus
607.	weekly	weakly	wekeley	weekeley
608.	differance	diferance	defference	difference

33

609.	sentence	sintince	centence	sentense
610.	citation	ceitation	citatetion	citetion
611.	equellly	equally	equiely	equelly
612.	lerature	literature	litereture	literashure
613.	rsponsible	responsible	respunsible	responsibl
614.	ligibley	ligible	ligeble	legible
615.	oven	ovien	ovain	oveen
616.	neturelly	naturally	neturally	naterely
617.	batttle	bettle	batle	battle
618.	milshekee	mikshaeke	milkshake	milshake
619.	enturpirse	enturprice	entirpraise	enterprise
620.	gorela	gorilla	gurella	grillla
621.	giraffe	geiraffe	geiraffe	geriffe
622.	qualetiy	qualiety	qualety	quality
623.	rinoceros	rhinoceros	rhneoceros	rheneros
624.	Africa	Afreica	Affrica	Affreca
625.	sientist	scientast	sceinstist	scientist
626.	poletic	politick	pulitic	politics
627.	nutrishionist	newtritionest	natritionest	nutritionist

628.	barrel	barel	borrel	berrel
629.	idaentify	identeify	idientify	identify
630.	supermarkit	supermerket	supermarket	suppermarket
631.	transmession	transmssion	trensmission	transmission
632.	hgiene	hygiene	higene	hygen
633.	Georgia	Gorgia	Goergia	Giorgia
634.	advencement	advanscement	advancement	advincement
635.	particulir	partecular	particular	parcular
636.	ombrella	umbrella	umbrila	umbraela
637.	wholesale	wholelsele	holesale	whoulsele
638.	agression	aggression	aggreson	aggrassion
639.	achevement	acheivement	achievement	acheevement
640.	fundamentally	fondamentally	fandamentally	fundmentally
641.	accountible	accountable	acountable	accauntable
642.	breakfast	brakefast	breakfest	breakfst
643.	hostage	hustege	houstage	hastage
644.	pumpken	pompkin	pumpkin	pumkin
645.	commercial	commerial	comercial	cummercial
646.	expadite	expidite	axpedite	expedite

647.	trilions	trileions	trillons	trillions
648.	massaje	massage	masage	masaje
649.	selebrate	celebrite	celebrat	celebrate
650.	accumplish	akcomplish	acomplish	accomplish
651.	xpension	expansion	expanshon	exxpansoin
652.	visionery	vesesinry	visionary	vesonary
653.	globel	globla	glubal	global
654.	comon	commun	common	cummon
655.	commitmeant	comitmant	commitment	committment
656.	president	presidant	presidint	presedent
657.	famaely	fameley	familey	family
658.	announce	announse	anuonce	announse
659.	announcement	annancement	anouncement	announcemint
660.	pronuncieation	pronunsiation	pronunceiation	pronunciation
661.	aticulate	articalate	arteiculate	articulate
662.	secuondary	sekondary	secondary	secundary
663.	envieronmental	incremental	environmental	environental
664.	democratic	demecratick	demokratick	demiocratic
665.	aucktion	auction	aacktion	aucshion

666.	Masscuhsesste	Massechuesset	Massachusetts	Matchuset
667.	adetion	adition	additoin	addition
668.	bulletin	bulletain	bolletin	bullatin
669.	sanetozer	sanitizer	senetizer	sanityzer
670.	orgenel	oregenial	original	oreginel
671.	crysteel	crysteal	crestal	crystal
672.	geographic	geografic	geographec	gerographic
673.	nashional	nuational	national	netional
674.	diliver	delaver	deliver	delivur
675.	undrline	underlane	undirline	underline
676.	wirrelass	wireless	whireles	wiireliss
677.	protection	protaction	protecshion	protecon
678.	konfidense	confeidence	counfidence	confidence
679.	sircumstences	curcumstances	circumstances	circumstnces
680.	world	wurld	wourld	wordl
681.	erth	eurth	earht	earth
682.	copereation	coperation	cooparation	cooperation
683.	substatute	substitute	substitate	substitote
684.	atidute	atitude	attitude	attitute

685.	pageant	pajeant	pagent	pageaint
686.	sertifecation	certification	certicashon	cirtificaton
687.	crypt	criypt	cryppt	cript
688.	employmeat	empluyment	employmint	employment
689.	annual	anual	annaul	annuel
690.	combination	cumbination	combenation	combinaton
691.	foreing	foureing	foreign	foregn
692.	companion	compaenion	companoin	companon
693.	abundent	aboundant	abundeant	abundant
694.	resource	resorce	resuorce	risource
695.	almanack	almanac	almenec	allmanace
696.	weathr	waether	weather	wether
697.	deicision	decision	dicision	decison
698.	stedium	staduim	stadium	stadum
699.	constitution	constituton	constetution	konsitution
700.	nattionelity	nationality	netionalitly	nationlity
701.	guarantee	guarante	guarentee	guarante
702.	directon	direction	diraection	diraction
703.	watermelon	watermaon	wathermelon	wadermelon

704.	Febrerey	February	Fabruary	Febraury
705.	pressare	pressure	prissure	presure
706.	deictation	dicteation	dictation	diction
707.	spculation	speculation	spiculation	specultion
708.	litegation	ligeitation	letegation	litigation
709.	secton	section	secshon	secktion
710.	liquidetion	liquidetion	lequidation	liquidation
711.	experience	experiense	experiensce	xpereince
712.	delite	delight	delihgt	dilight
713.	Australian	Australien	Astralian	Austrelian
714.	embarrased	embarrassid	emberressed	embarrassed
715.	specifick	specific	spacefic	speciphic
716.	journel	jarnel	juornel	journal
717.	babuon	baboon	babooon	beboon
718.	appreciation	appresiation	apreciation	apprecation
719.	censitive	sensitave	sensative	sensitive
720.	musicel	musical	mousical	musickal
721.	entertanment	entertainment	entirtainment	entertanment
722.	risearch	resaerch	researsh	research

723.	pertan	purtain	pertain	pertane
724.	selalective	silective	selective	selectave
725.	hybernate	hibernate	hibirnate	hybirnete
726.	shappoo	shampoo	shempoo	shampo
727.	powerful	powrful	powerfull	pawerful
728.	mariiage	mariage	marriage	merriage
729.	rehearsel	rihersal	rehearsal	rehaersal
730.	Louisiana	Lousaina	Lusiana	Louesiana
731.	Antarctica	Anarticak	Anertica	Anarteca
732.	Hemisphare	Hemisphere	Hamispharre	Hemisfere
733.	Equator	Equater	Equetor	Equatir
734.	Arjgentina	Argenteina	Argintina	Argentina
735.	rimnent	reamnant	remnant	rimnent
736.	connection	connecton	cunnection	conection
737.	internet	intarnet	internit	internaet
738.	consigment	consignment	consigmint	consegnment
739.	impression	impresion	imprassion	imprission
740.	hamburger	hemberger	hemburger	hambarger
741.	Conecticut	Konnectict	Cunnecticuat	Connecticut

742.	adittion	addition	adition	addishon
743.	birthdae	birthday	burthday	berthday
744.	sleeveless	sleveliss	sleeeveless	sleaveless
745.	practise	practisce	pracktise	practice
746.	gretist	greatest	graetest	greatist
747.	Geographic	Gegraphic	Goiegraphic	Geoibgrfic
748.	intirpretation	interpraetation	interpretetion	interpretation
749.	semplify	simplify	simplefy	simpilify
750.	underlane	underline	undline	undirline
751.	strenght	strangth	strength	stringth
752.	protaction	pruction	protection	protecton
753.	confidance	confedence	confideance	confidence
754.	circustaences	circumstences	curcumstances	circumstances
755.	house	huose	hause	hous
756.	homograph	homofraph	homogreph	homograf
757.	speling	spelling	spalling	spellin
758.	shepherd	shaphird	shepheard	shapherd
759.	attiude	atitude	attitud	attitude
760.	miserable	meiserable	miserabel	maseriable

761.	reedeble	raedable	readable	readebel
762.	keangaroo	kangarooo	kengarou	kangaroo
763.	coyoates	coyotas	koyotes	coyotes
764.	mammal	mammel	memmal	mamal
765.	Janaury	January	Janewrary	Janaur
766.	purpel	pirpule	purplle	purple
767.	Decimber	Decembir	December	Diciember
768.	resoluton	resolution	risolution	resulution
769.	cunfetti	confette	confetti	confeti
770.	constame	constoome	cunstome	costume
771.	keybard	keyboard	kayboard	keybaord
772.	television	televisoin	talavesion	telivision
773.	graphec	grephic	graphic	grafic
774.	fantestick	fantastic	fanntastic	fentastic
775.	dramaetic	dramatic	dramatick	drammatic
776.	accelerate	acelerate	acelerate	accelerat
777.	cabage	cabege	cabbaje	cabbage
778.	recognize	recognice	recognise	recagnize
779.	alteration	alteritation	alteretion	altaration

780.	minimize	minnimize	meinimize	minamize
781.	representaton	rapresentation	representation	represetation
782.	tradetionel	traditional	traditionel	treditional
783.	Virgenia	Verginia	Virginea	Virginia
784.	wonderful	wondirful	wonderfull	wanderful
785.	riduction	reducktion	raduction	reduction
786.	practikal	precticel	practical	practikel
787.	administration	admenistration	adminestretion	admenstraton
788.	enhancement	enhancemant	inhancment	enhancemint
789.	campen	campaign	campaignen	cempgaign
790.	investigetion	investigation	invastigation	invistigation
791.	gestaure	gasture	gesture	jesture
792.	sulicitation	solicetaiotn	solicitation	soulliciation
793.	Talahasseee	Tallahassee	Tallahasea	Tallehassee
794.	Missipie	Mississippy	Misissipi	Mississippi
795.	prioritize	prioritise	pryiritize	prortize
796.	perpendicular	perpandecular	purpindicular	perpindiculer
797.	examanetion	examination	exeminaiton	examenation
798.	critecal	critical	kritical	cretical

43

799.	govermint	guvernment	governmant	government
800.	cicle	cyclle	cylcle	cycle
801.	trensfar	transfir	transfer	transfur
802.	bankrapt	bankrupt	bankrup	bunkrupt
803.	colapse	collepse	collapsse	collapse
804.	stampeede	stemped	stampeed	stampede
805.	gorella	gorilla	gurella	gorila
806.	scripshure	scriptuare	scripture	scrapture
807.	candedate	canddidatae	candidate	kandidate
808.	speech	speach	sppech	speesh
809.	balerina	ballerina	ballirina	ballerena
810.	reguleton	regulation	reguletion	regulaton
811.	residence	resadense	residense	resedence
812.	difrost	deafrost	dfraust	defrost
813.	pacture	picckture	picture	picshure
814.	sagnature	signetue	signeture	signature
815.	ceremeic	ceramick	ceremic	ceramic
816.	instell	installl	instaul	install
817.	coplicate	complicate	completcate	complecete

818.	grapefruit	greapfruit	grapfruit	grepfrut
819.	keew	kiwi	kiwii	kiiwii
820.	improvamint	improvement	emprovement	improvmint
821.	iresponsibel	irrisponsibel	irresponsible	irresponsabel
822.	debat	debate	dbate	dibate
823.	educatir	educetaor	educetor	educator
824.	choas	kaos	khaos	chaos
825.	appearance	apperence	appaerance	aperance
826.	finjerneil	fingurnale	fingernail	fengernaile
827.	Ibrow	Ibraw	eiyebraow	eyebrow
828.	Canadien	Canadian	Cenedian	Canaedian
829.	alternator	alternatur	alternatr	alternatir
830.	rootine	routene	routin	routine
831.	coverage	coverag	covarag	coverege
832.	paiyment	paymint	peymant	payment
833.	transparincy	trensperancy	transperancey	transparency
834.	children	childran	childrun	chidrin
835.	llinoiss	llenois	Illinios	Illinois
836.	recomind	recomend	recommind	recommend

837.	physicen	physyician	physician	physcian
838.	techneican	technicien	tachnician	technician
839.	anneverary	anniversery	aniversary	anniversary
840.	Afghanistan	Afganistan	Afghenestan	Afganistan
841.	ferret	feret	ferreit	ferett
842.	Pennsylavaniea	Pennsylvania	Pensylvania	Pennslvania
843.	electrick	electrac	eliectric	electric
844.	steadium	stedium	stadium	stedum
845.	aprum	aprun	apronn	apron
846.	retailur	retailir	retialer	retailer
847.	electrician	eletrecian	elictrican	elecktrian
848.	reporter	reportier	repourtir	repurter
849.	inteligent	intelligent	enteligint	intellegint
850.	veterian	viteran	veterun	veteran
851.	prosecutor	prasecutor	procecutor	prosacutor
852.	Alaska	Aleska	Alaskua	Alascka
853.	demolich	demolash	dmolish	demolish
854.	accuseciton	accusation	acusation	accusetion
855.	treatment	treamint	treatmint	traetment

856.	priority	pryority	prirety	prorety
857.	chaurity	charety	charity	charitee
858.	potateo	ptatoe	potato	puotato
859.	hedlight	headlite	haedlight	headlight
860.	pruogram	progrem	prougram	program
861.	volcenoe	volcano	vulcanoe	volnoe
862.	exploude	xplode	explodde	explode
863.	magnificent	magneificent	magnefisent	magnifecent
864.	kilogram	kelogram	kilgram	kilagram
865.	destructive	disktructive	distructive	destrucktive
866.	productive	producktive	prodactive	produtive
867.	cautiousely	cautisly	cautiously	cautoiuisly
868.	easily	easeley	easilly	eeasily
869.	accidant	accidennt	acident	accident
870.	pronounce	pronunce	pronuonce	prounce
871.	pirpose	purpose	prpose	purposse
872.	risearch	research	resarch	riserach
873.	comune	kommune	cummune	commune
874.	ostrach	ustrich	ostrische	ostrich

875.	searching	searshing	serching	serchang
876.	humingbrid	hummingbird	hammingbard	hammigbird
877.	underground	udergruond	undergraund	undergraound
878.	perphume	pirfume	perfume	perfum
879.	invalid	invelid	invaleed	invalide
880.	futurae	phuture	fouture	future
881.	discherg	discharge	descharje	descharge
882.	inseurt	insurt	insert	insart
883.	entrence	endrance	entrence	entrance
884.	demunstratation	demonstratin	demonstraetion	demonstration
885.	shield	sheild	chield	sheeld
886.	fountaine	fountein	fontain	fountain
887.	classic	clasick	clessick	classcik
888.	sciense	science	sceoince	scienc
889.	Washengton	Weshington	Washington	Washenton
890.	mainten	menten	menntain	maintain
891.	pirsuade	persuade	peisaude	persuede
892.	persuasion	persuaseion	persasaion	persuesion
893.	compleation	complition	cumplition	completion

894.	definition	defenetion	dfinition	difinition
895.	transfom	tranfurm	transform	tranform
896.	suppert	saport	suport	support
897.	evaaulte	evalulte	evaluatte	evaluate
898.	caracter	character	cherecter	charctir
899.	publesher	publisher	poblisher	publasher
900.	suspenson	saspension	suspinsion	suspension
901.	museum	maseium	mucseum	mouseum
902.	skateboard	skatebard	sckteboard	sketeboard
903.	ofense	offense	offancse	offensce
904.	humiliation	humilietio	hamilation	houmiliation
905.	resantement	resentment	resintment	rasentment
906.	pruoficient	proficent	profecient	proficient
907.	hypir	hypur	hipier	hyper
908.	explain	explane	explaine	explene
909.	fruite	fruit	froot	frout
910.	bannnana	banana	bannanna	bananna
911.	soccker	soccar	soccer	soccir
912.	daffodel	dofodil	daffodil	doffidil

913.	bhavior	behavioer	behevior	behavior
914.	yesterday	yesturday	yestirday	yisterday
915.	musician	musishon	musicien	musiceian
916.	sobmarine	submarine	submerine	submareine
917.	quentity	quantety	quentity	quantity
918.	minute	minetute	minate	minutte
919.	respact	rispect	respecct	respect
920.	plumbor	plambor	plumber	plubir
921.	ovan	ovin	ovun	oven
922.	toastier	toster	toastur	toaster
923.	microwave	microsweve	mickrowave	microweve
924.	blendir	blender	blandur	blendor
925.	cyclinder	cylinder	cinlinder	cylander
926.	levender	lavender	lanvindir	lanvender
927.	vioilet	violet	violat	violit
928.	rhinestone	rhanestone	rihestune	rhineastoune
929.	grenelate	granewlated	granulated	granuulated
930.	dassy	daisy	diasy	deisy
931.	height	heightt	heiht	heigt

932.	ignourance	ignarance	ignorence	ignorance
933.	immediate	imedieate	immadiate	imediate
934.	humorous	humoras	humorouass	humourus
935.	jewalry	jewelry	jewalry	julwerly
936.	juadgament	judgment	judgamint	judgemant
937.	librerey	librarey	library	liebrary
938.	licanse	lecense	liceanse	license
939.	millnnium	millanium	millennium	mallenium
940.	miniatare	menetature	miniature	menetaure
941.	maintenense	maintenence	manetenance	maintenance
942.	principal	princapel	prencipal	princepel
943.	questionnaire	questionnare	questonnair	qustionnaire
944.	refered	referred	referrad	referrred
945.	referense	referanse	reference	repherence
946.	rhymea	rihyme	rhym	rhyme
947.	schedule	sckedule	skedule	schadule
948.	vackuum	vacuum	vecuum	vacuumm
949.	souvenar	souvnier	souvenir	soviner
950.	pamplets	pamphlets	pamphlats	pamphlits

51

951.	particulir	particular	partecular	particuler
952.	opioin	upion	openion	opinion
953.	ocassionally	occasionely	occasionally	occasoinally
954.	purmenentt	permanent	purmanent	pirmanent
955.	sylabale	syllabele	syllebel	syllable
956.	tendansy	tendency	tendancy	tendensy
957.	fluor	flour	fluore	flouir
958.	speciefecally	specefecally	spacifically	specifically
959.	symmetrical	symmetraticl	symmetrecal	simmetrical
960.	stretejy	stratagey	strategy	stretegy
961.	cincerely	sincerely	sinceraley	sincarely
962.	withdrawaul	withdrawal	wethdrawl	wethdrawal
963.	outrageous	outrageus	outregous	outrageuos
964.	prescraption	prescription	prescrapton	priscription
965.	straggle	strugle	struggel	struggle
966.	championship	championsshep	cheampionship	champonship
967.	bussiness	busness	beesiness	business
968.	hyproacrate	hiprocrite	hypocrite	hyprocrit
969.	courtesy	cortesty	courtasy	courtasey

970.	character	cherecter	charecter	charackter
971.	characteristic	charecteristick	cherectareistic	charactaristac
972.	criticaze	criticize	critiecize	creticize
973.	infermation	information	informetion	infurmation
974.	interrapt	interaupt	interupt	interrupt
975.	iland	ilend	islaend	island
976.	exaggerate	exagerat	exaggeraete	exagerate
977.	enimey	enemy	enemie	enamey
978.	benifciel	beneficial	benefshial	benefecial
979.	compenion	companin	companion	cumpenion
980.	desperate	disperete	disperate	desperete
981.	appearence	apperence	appearance	aperance
982.	accommodate	accommmodate	accomodate	accomudate
983.	ameture	amateur	amatur	ammateur
984.	address	adress	adress	addrass
985.	megezine	magazine	megesine	magazin
986.	rection	reacton	reacktion	reaction
987.	clerification	clarifcetion	clarification	clerefication
988.	laburatory	laboratory	lebouratory	laboretry

989.	lieutenent	lietenant	lieutenant	lietnant
990.	controversal	cuntrovrercial	contruversial	controversial
991.	Saptimber	Septimber	September	Septembur
992.	perjury	purjury	pirjary	pirjaury
993.	ordinery	ordenery	ordinary	ourdinary
994.	decreese	decreas	decrease	dcrease
995.	anniverseary	anniversary	aniversery	anneversery
996.	peaceful	peacefull	peaful	peaseful
997.	appropriate	approprete	apropriate	appropriete
998.	propuerty	proputy	property	proparty
999.	suggist	suggast	sugest	suggest
1000.	offise	offiace	offace	office
1001.	furmer	former	formir	furmur
1002.	authir	author	auther	authier
1003.	governor	gavornir	governr	gouverner
1004.	famielier	familer	familiar	femiliar
1005.	bizere	bizarre	bizare	bizzere
1006.	surreal	sureal	surreel	surael
1007.	realize	realise	reliaze	realice

1008.	corner	cornur	cornor	korner
1009.	opshon	option	uption	opshion
1010.	impeachment	impeachmient	empeechment	impechment
1011.	conference	conferece	confarance	cunfarence
1012.	creditebelety	credetibility	creditbability	credibility
1013.	politically	poletically	politicaly	puletically
1014.	situaton	setueation	situashon	situation
1015.	accose	accuse	ackuse	accusse
1016.	mervelous	marvelous	marvalous	marvelos
1017.	fource	phorce	force	forcce
1018.	articel	artickle	article	artecle
1019.	opinon	upinion	opinion	opinon
1020.	effective	effactive	efective	effactive
1021.	railroad	railrode	ralroad	rialroad
1022.	interast	interest	intirist	enterest
1023.	reqire	require	riquire	reqiare
1024.	elecshion	eletion	election	ilection
1025.	selecton	selection	seletion	seleshon
1026.	kapable	capabel	capablle	capable

1027.	bcause	bekause	becuase	because
1028.	syllable	sylable	syllabel	cyllable
1029.	memorial	mimorial	mamorial	memurial
1030.	extinded	extended	xtended	extendid
1031.	seasonel	seasonal	seesonal	ceasonal
1032.	Haloween	Haulloween	Halloween	Halowen
1033.	Enjlish	English	Englash	Englissh
1034.	emotionel	emutional	emotonal	emotional
1035.	deelership	dealirship	delearship	dealership
1036.	sympathy	sympethee	simpethy	sympethie
1037.	sherif	sheriff	shariff	sharif
1038.	privacy	privecy	pravacy	privasee
1039.	securaity	sekurity	secarity	security
1040.	welthy	wealhy	wealty	wealthy
1041.	condomeneium	cundomium	condominium	conduminium
1042.	condetion	cundition	condition	condtion
1043.	concrite	concreat	cuncrete	concrete
1044.	conclusion	conklushon	concluson	conclushon
1045.	sense	sene	sence	cense

1046.	servant	servint	sirvnat	servunt
1047.	condetion	cundition	condition	condttion
1048.	thrlled	thriled	thrilled	thralled
1049.	arroma	aruoma	aroma	aromma
1050.	arrugant	arrogent	arrogant	arogant
1051.	eighteen	ateteen	eghteen	eighttin
1052.	purchese	purchase	pirchase	pirchese
1053.	proveke	provoke	provke	provuke
1054.	magnet	magnit	megnat	mugnet
1055.	machinery	machinary	mashinery	machiniry
1056.	instition	enstitution	instetution	institution
1057.	intilligent	intalligent	intelligant	intelligent
1058.	enstallment	instalment	installmint	installment
1059.	infiction	enfection	infecshon	infection
1060.	influence	influense	influince	infloence
1061.	modarat	moderate	muderate	modarate
1062.	queston	question	quistion	qeustion
1063.	raspbarry	rasbery	raspbery	raspberry
1064.	qeualification	qualefecetion	qalification	qualification

1065.	puzzle	pzzel	puzle	puzzel
1066.	swaemp	swemp	swamp	swmp
1067.	syrop	sirup	syrup	syroup
1068.	syringe	syrinje	syrange	syring
1069.	purse	purce	pursse	purs
1070.	verieties	varieties	varities	vareities
1071.	expence	expense	expens	xpense
1072.	expiere	expere	expire	expirre
1073.	intervew	inturview	interview	intirview
1074.	excose	excse	exkuse	excuse
1075.	advanse	advince	advance	advanc
1076.	accomplish	acomplish	acomplesh	accomplich
1077.	supportive	supportve	suppurtive	suportive
1078.	creatave	creative	createve	creetive
1079.	enjouy	enjoy	enjouy	engoy
1080.	communitei	community	comunity	cummunity
1081.	louggage	lujgage	luggege	luggage
1082.	grease	greese	greace	graese
1083.	ocurrence	occurrence	occurrance	ocurance

1084.	mispel	misspell	misspall	mispal
1085.	personel	pursonnel	personnel	persunnel
1086.	argoment	argumint	argument	agument
1087.	illiterate	illerite	illiterite	elliterate
1088.	absolutely	absulutely	absulotely	asolutely
1089.	statisticel	stetestical	statistical	statistecel
1090.	incliment	inclemint	incklement	inclement
1091.	pastkard	postcard	posstcerd	pstcurd
1092.	beleive	believe	beelieve	blieve
1093.	diescipline	desciplene	discipline	descipline
1094.	colun	colunm	column	culumn
1095.	colleckteble	cullectible	collictible	collectible
1096.	catagury	categury	category	catagary
1097.	recitel	resital	recital	ricitial
1098.	rebeeled	rebild	ribuild	rebuild
1099.	eequipmint	equipment	equipmint	equipmant
1100.	expirience	experience	experinse	experiense
1101.	ancetor	ancistor	ancestor	ancestur
1102.	selectave	selactive	selective	silective

1103.	semilar	similir	similur	similar
1104.	Maxico	Mexico	Mexiko	Mexaco
1105.	Colorado	Coluourado	Culorado	Coloradoe
1106.	Youtah	Utuah	Utah	Utauh
1107.	Road Iland	Rhode Iland	Rhode Island	Rode Islund
1108.	Europe	Eurpae	Euroupe	Eurupe
1109.	France	Franse	Francce	Fransce
1110.	tranfurm	transform	transfourm	trensform
1111.	establishmint	estableshment	establishment	estableishmint
1112.	orchistra	orchestraw	orchestra	orchistra
1113.	aspieretion	aspiretion	aspiration	aspirashion
1114.	expresion	exppression	expression	xprission
1115.	enargy	eneirgy	energee	energy
1116.	Michigan	Michegan	Mechegean	Michigen
1117.	Detriot	Detroit	Ditroit	Dtrout
1118.	eficiency	efficiency	effenciency	eficeincy
1119.	convence	cunvince	convience	convince
1120.	failshure	fialure	failure	failore
1121.	hundrad	hundrid	hondred	hundred

1122.	simoltaneously	simultanesly	simultaneously	simulteneosly
1123.	engage	engege	engeje	engaje
1124.	aproach	approach	approoch	appraoch
1125.	detirmine	determine	determaine	determin
1126.	queston	questoin	question	qustion
1127.	pirpose	purpuse	purpose	purposse
1128.	outlyne	ouline	outlinne	outline
1129.	vigilent	vagilant	vigilint	vigilant
1130.	kommand	cummund	comand	command
1131.	dangerous	dangerus	dengarous	dangirous
1132.	anticipate	antecepate	anticipete	anticipat
1133.	potentel	potential	putential	potantial
1134.	copycet	copycut	copycat	caopcat
1135.	entellijence	intillegance	intelligence	inteligance
1136.	effectave	effactive	effective	efective
1137.	prissure	presure	presshure	pressure
1138.	primery	paimary	premery	primary
1139.	security	securatity	secaraty	securitay
1140.	progrss	progriss	prograss	progress

1141.	Arkanses	Arkansas	Arkenses	Arkinsis
1142.	Minesota	Minnesota	Minneseta	Minssota
1143.	deadline	dedline	deadlune	daedline
1144.	destract	destract	deistract	distract
1145.	compromise	comprommise	cumpromice	compramise
1146.	fregrance	fragrence	fragrance	fragranse
1147.	importent	important	emporantnt	impourtant
1148.	capeigne	campaign	campiagnne	campaoign
1149.	Brazil	Brezel	Brizal	Brazal
1150.	Venezueela	Venaezuela	Vienezuela	Venezuela
1151.	incmplete	imcomplete	encomplet	incomplete
1152.	nspere	enspire	inspaire	inspire
1153.	triggir	triger	trigger	triggar
1154	detacheble	ditecheble	detachable	ditashable
1155.	forehead	fourehad	forheead	forhed
1156.	measure	measshure	mesure	maeshure
1157.	describe	dascribe	descrabe	discribe
1158.	chaljenge	challenge	challiege	chalengke
1159.	manajer	maneger	manasher	manager

1160.	stepler	stapllur	stapler	staplir
1161.	sure	shoor	shure	chure
1162.	rusj	raoush	rosh	rush
1163.	wheles	whaeles	whales	whules
1164.	vanella	vanille	veneilla	vanilla
1165.	strawberry	strawburry	strewberry	struwberry
1166.	flavour	flavor	flevour	flavuor
1167.	stranjer	stranger	strenger	straunger
1168.	reacshion	reacton	reaction	raection
1169.	humalate	humalite	humiliate	humeleate
1170.	exhaussted	exhusted	exhausted	xhausted
1171.	congraultions	cungratlations	congratulations	cungratulatons
1172.	rebound	rbound	rebaund	reboand
1173.	melnutrition	malnutretion	malnewtrition	malnutrition
1174.	marroied	married	maried	marrieed
1175.	psychologist	pischologiest	pyscholagiest	sychologest
1176.	optometrist	optomitrist	optomatirst	uptommetrist
1177.	flece	fleece	fleese	fleace
1178.	dentaist	dintist	dentist	dantest

1179.	dieticen	dietiten	dietishon	dietitian
1180.	contry	countrary	country	cuontry
1181.	sympathy	simpathy	symputhy	sympethy
1182.	removable	remuveble	rimovable	rimovoable
1183.	Januarei	Junauary	January	Januarie
1184.	sheken	shakin	shaken	shacken
1185.	cruisse	cruse	criuse	cruise
1186.	beautisian	beautican	beatician	beautician
1187.	triathlon	triathlun	thrialon	tryathlon
1188.	urigienel	original	oregenal	origenal
1189.	geoperdy	jeoperdy	jeopurdy	jeopardy
1190.	academic	academaic	akcademec	acakedemic
1191.	vital	vetel	vytal	vatal
1192.	hedache	headache	haedaceh	headach
1193.	esophagus	esophegus	esuphagus	easophagus
1194.	masterpece	mastirpiece	masterpiece	mesterpiece
1195.	flamboyant	flambouyant	flaboyent	flamboyent
1196.	febrick	fabric	fabrick	fabreck
1197.	passon	pasion	passion	passhon

1198.	imaje	emage	image	imege
1199.	instrement	instrament	instrument	enstrument
1200.	wardrobe	wardroube	werdrboe	wardrube
1201.	retrever	retrieever	retriever	ritreivur
1202.	Colie	Cullied	Kollie	Collie
1203.	Borzoi	Burzoi	Borzio	Birzoi
1204.	Speniel	Spaniel	Spanoiel	Spanal
1205.	appreciete	apprecete	appreciate	appriciete
1206.	retirement	retirment	retiremant	retiremint
1207.	vempire	vampere	vampire	vampiere
1208.	sweatir	sweter	sweater	swaeter
1209.	pulyester	polyester	polyaster	polyestir
1210.	radient	reedient	radent	radiant
1211.	sirculate	curculatee	circelate	circulate
1212.	clevier	clevar	clevur	clever
1213.	sheepdog	sheepdag	shepdog	sheeepdog
1214.	buffalo	buffalow	buffaloo	bufale
1215.	beever	beaver	beavier	baever
1216.	bager	budger	badger	badgur

1217.	anteloop	antaloupe	anteloup	antelope
1218.	camel	cumel	camle	camal
1219.	buzard	buzzard	buzzerd	bazzard
1220.	penguin	pengen	pengin	pinquin
1221.	perot	parrot	perrot	parot
1222.	hinea	hyene	hyena	hyne
1223.	porcoupine	porcupine	porkcupine	porcupain
1224.	weasell	weassel	wheasel	weasel
1225.	mayor	meyer	mayir	mayour
1226.	tarantula	tarentula	taratola	tarentela
1227.	zeep kode	zeip cude	zip code	zipp codde
1228.	company	cumpany	copany	cumpenie
1229.	gimnasium	gymnesum	gymnasium	gimnesium
1230.	diduction	deduction	daduction	dedution
1231.	oshean	oshon	ocien	ocean
1232.	nourshmant	nourishment	nourishmint	nourrashment
1233.	nutrition	nutration	nutrishon	nutriton
1234.	iluminate	iluminete	illuminate	ellumineate
1235.	enclose	inclose	encloase	enclase

1236.	karaoke	kaoake	caraoke	karoke
1237.	shouldir	shoulder	shaolder	shalder
1238.	tradaed	treded	treded	traded
1239.	propouse	propase	propose	prepose
1240.	advise	advase	aadvise	addvise
1241.	quaelified	qualified	queilifed	qulifed
1242.	agrement	agreemant	agreemint	agreement
1243.	wrong	wrang	whrang	wong
1244.	pramises	premeses	premiases	premises
1245.	evakusate	evaicuate	evacuate	evacaute
1246.	solushon	soulation	soluton	solution
1247.	privae	privete	private	prifate
1248.	kangeraoo	kangaroo	cangaroo	kengaroo
1249.	elevator	alevator	elivatur	elevatur
1250.	escalator	eskalator	esscalator	ascalator
1251.	elavate	elevate	elivate	alavate
1252.	apointmen	appointmin	appioment	appointment
1253.	dinstriy	dentisttry	dantastry	dentistry
1254.	from	phrom	frum	frem

1255.	whan	wen	when	whin
1256.	whish	whiach	whach	which
1257.	each	ech	eech	aech
1258.	know	knaw	kow	knouw
1259.	whater	water	wather	watur
1260.	calcalator	calculatur	calculator	calculatir
1261.	second	secaond	sekond	sacond
1262.	stealion	stellion	stallion	stalion
1263.	exemple	exampel	exempal	example
1264.	towaed	toward	touward	towerd
1265.	hemself	hyimself	himself	hymself
1266.	nicklice	nacklase	neklase	necklace
1267.	surface	surphace	sirface	sarface
1268.	vioce	voicce	voice	voce
1269.	excaepe	escap	iscaspe	escape
1270.	rehabilitation	rehabilitashon	rihabilation	rehabelitaton
1271.	identifcetion	identification	identifcation	idantification
1272.	connecton	conection	connaction	connection
1273.	amezine	amazeing	amazing	amezing

1274.	trampoline	trampooline	trempoline	trampline
1275.	distenction	distinction	distancion	distanction
1276.	coupel	couple	cauople	kouple
1277.	hendsom	handsum	handsome	hansom
1278.	novelty	nouvilty	novilty	naovelty
1279.	mimorable	mamorable	memorable	memurable
1280.	nevegate	navigeate	navigate	navigete
1281.	kolesterol	cholesterol	colesteral	cholasteral
1282.	chikan	chickin	checken	chicken
1283.	package	packege	pakege	packeje
1284.	damage	demege	damaje	damege
1285.	deodorent	deodorant	dedorant	doedorant
1286.	leadershap	leedership	laedershap	leadership
1287.	douonation	donashion	danation	donation
1288.	juice	jiuce	guice	juce
1289.	international	internetionel	enternational	nternational
1290.	aerlly	early	urly	arly
1291.	kaetchup	keitchup	ketchop	ketchup
1292.	Pearis	Parris	Pariss	Paris

1293.	benner	bunner	baner	banner
1294.	season	seeson	seasin	seasan
1295.	instrument	instrament	enstrument	nstrament
1296.	cheampion	champon	champen	champion
1297.	dapick	depick	depict	dapict
1298.	paytron	patrun	patron	pattron
1299.	tamatoes	tomatoes	tometoes	toematoes
1300.	ngredent	ingredient	engredeint	ingradient
1301.	sheeld	chield	shaled	shield
1302.	Equetor	Equator	Equatir	Equeter
1303.	presenter	presintr	presantir	prasenter
1304.	identifay	endentify	indentify	identify
1305.	extrameley	extremely	extremily	extremeely
1306.	opnion	opineoun	opinion	upinion
1307.	unikue	uniqk	unik	unique
1308.	postpune	postpone	postpane	poustpone
1309.	applcant	applicint	applicant	aplicent
1310.	remender	reiminder	reminder	riminder
1311.	eckonomy	economy	aconomy	econamy

1312.	acceisble	accessible	accessibel	acceisible
1313.	averaje	averaje	averege	average
1314.	consigmint	consignment	consignmant	consigmint
1315.	allergic	allergac	alergic	allergick
1316.	arthritis	arthretes	artritis	arthretis
1317.	fierce	feirce	fierrce	fierse
1318.	maneuvar	maneuver	manuerver	manuver
1319.	suspeicious	suspicius	suspecious	suspicious
1320.	detectave	detictive	detectife	detective
1321.	exquisiete	exquiseat	exquisite	esquisite
1322.	revesion	revison	rivision	revision
1323.	consequence	consequeance	consequance	consiquence
1324.	disinfected	disinfacted	disanfected	disinficted
1325.	ballestic	ballistick	ballisteck	ballistic
1326.	eligable	eligible	eligibel	eligibal
1327.	entrigued	intrigued	intreguick	intriguied
1328.	invesion	invasion	invasoin	infasion
1329.	defeint	difaint	defiant	defint
1330.	hideos	hideous	heedious	hideuos

1331.	discremination	discremenation	discrimination	descriemination
1332.	therapeutic	therapeutick	therepeutic	theraputic
1333.	resumme	resume	resiume	risume
1334.	transplant	treasplant	tresplant	transplent
1335.	transiente	transient	transeint	trensient
1336.	vinditict	vindictive	vindactive	vindictave
1337.	peaches	peeches	paeches	peachies
1338.	experience	expereince	expirence	expirience
1339.	conclusion	conclusoin	conclosion	conclushon
1340.	delibiritately	deliberetely	deliberataly	deliberately
1341.	intarrupting	intirrupting	interrupting	interropting
1342.	mysterios	mysterias	mystarious	mysterious
1343.	snetching	snatching	snutching	snautching
1344.	extansion	extenshion	extinsion	extension
1345.	Milwaukee	Milkwaukee	Milwaokey	Milwaukey
1346.	obnoxous	ubnoxious	obnuxious	obnoxious
1347.	conviction	cunviction	convicktion	convection
1348.	canuppy	canopy	cenopy	cunopy
1349.	slevery	slaviry	slavery	slavary

1350.	believe	beleive	beliave	blieve
1351.	monay	moneay	mouney	money
1352.	penne	penny	panny	pennny
1353.	quartir	qurter	quarter	querter
1354.	nickle	nickel	nickal	nickelk
1355.	insurance	inshurance	insurence	insuriance
1356.	arsoun	arsun	rson	arson
1357.	bogus	bougus	bogas	bogis
1358.	sufocate	suffokcate	suffokate	suffocate
1359.	sucumb	sucumb	succum	succumb
1360.	similerities	similarities	simalaraties	similereties
1361.	polynomeal	polynumial	polynomeil	polynomial
1362.	diminutive	dimanutave	diminuteve	dimenutive
1363.	anonymous	anonimous	anonemous	anonymos
1364.	fluoriscient	fluorescent	florescent	floriscient
1365.	microfelm	microfalm	micrkofilm	microfilm
1366.	eccentrick	eccentric	eccintrick	eccantric
1367.	volumine	volume	valume	voluume
1368.	debriss	dabris	debries	debris

1369.	charitable	charetible	charetable	chariteble
1370.	perimiter	perimeteor	perimeter	paraimeter
1371.	vybrate	vibrate	vibreate	fibrate
1372.	nuggets	nuggits	noggets	nugets
1373.	produsce	pruduce	produce	produse
1374.	alimuny	alimony	alemony	allimony
1375.	resedue	resedo	residu	residue
1376.	porcelane	porcelaine	porcilain	porcelain
1377.	camouflaje	camoflage	camouflage	camouflege
1378.	canter	cantur	cannter	cannter
1379.	coincedance	coincidence	cioncidence	coincedince
1380.	skiptical	skaptical	skeptecel	skeptical
1381.	pridator	preditor	predatour	predator
1382.	fierse	feirce	ferce	fierce
1383.	gratitudde	gratetude	greatitude	gratitude
1384.	negotiate	negosheate	negogaite	negogate
1385.	conflect	conflict	conflickt	cunflict
1386.	indicetor	indicatur	indicator	indicatir
1387.	scripture	scriptuore	scriptore	screpture

1388.	properity	prosperity	prusperity	prospirity
1389.	marsupial	marsopial	marsupeil	masupial
1390.	ancestir	ancestor	ancistor	ancector
1391.	geniration	genaration	generetion	generation
1392.	renovate	rinovate	rennovate	renuvete
1393.	stabilise	stebilize	stabilize	stabelize
1394.	parshal	partial	partail	paurtial
1395.	aggressave	aggressive	aggresseve	agressive
1396.	damaje	damage	damege	demege
1397.	coloni	colonny	coloney	colony
1398.	wurst	worst	wrst	worrst
1399.	parede	paradde	parde	parade
1400.	potential	poutenial	potenteil	potintial
1401.	carousel	karousel	carusel	caruosel
1402.	exircise	exarcise	exercise	excisses
1403.	alphebet	alfabet	alphebit	alphabet
1404.	cooperative	coopiritive	coopirative	cooparative
1405.	lotion	lotoin	loshon	lution
1406.	penut	peanut	pnut	peanot

1407.	delivery	delevery	dilivery	dlivery
1408.	emptee	ampty	empty	emty
1409.	mirror	mirrror	mirrir	merror
1410.	blding	building	biulding	bilding
1411.	envelope	envalope	envaloupe	envilope
1412.	instent	enstant	instant	instunt
1413.	senister	sinester	sinesster	sinister
1414.	pastryi	passtry	pastree	pastry
1415.	chocolait	chocoulate	chocolate	chokolate
1416.	ticket	tickat	tickit	tickete
1417.	squirril	squirrel	squerrel	squirel
1418.	preseon	prisun	prison	prisson
1419.	newstand	newssand	newsstand	knewssand
1420.	score	scure	sckore	scoure
1421.	newpapir	newspaper	newspeper	newspapur
1422.	learne	laern	lurn	learn
1423.	parient	parant	parent	perent
1424.	biagraphy	biogrephy	biography	biografy
1425.	cumpare	compare	compere	compre

1426.	explene	explian	expline	explain
1427.	narrative	narrateve	narretive	naratiive
1428.	descriptive	decriptave	descreptive	descreaptive
1429.	describ	discribe	deskribe	describe
1430.	tennis	tenis	tennes	tenniss
1431.	gleance	glance	glunce	glanse
1432.	poch	poach	poash	paoch
1433.	punctuetion	ponctuation	puncktuation	punctuation
1434.	riddle	riddel	ridle	reddle
1435.	pulite	polite	poulite	polight
1436.	disastros	desestrous	disastrous	disastrus
1437.	insect	insact	insict	inseck
1438.	Texis	Texaas	Txas	Texas
1439.	chane	chian	chain	chene
1440.	presedent	president	prisident	presidint
1441.	dimpele	dimple	demple	dimpel
1442.	surgiry	sirgery	surgery	srgery
1443.	doctor	doctur	docktor	doctir
1444.	dignitary	dignetery	dignitery	degnetary

1445.	struggle	strugegle	struggel	stroggle
1446.	exageration	exaggeration	exagiration	exaggeretion
1447.	humor	humour	homour	humir
1448.	language	languaje	lenjuage	lenguage
1449.	ciren	sirin	syiren	siren
1450.	technology	tecknology	technaology	technalogy
1451.	customir	customer	costomer	custaumer
1452.	morning	murning	monrning	morneng
1453.	Caleforneia	Califournia	California	Californea
1454.	dialolog	dielog	dialugue	dialogue
1455.	apostruphe	apostrophe	apostrofe	apustrophe
1456.	perentheses	parinthesis	parenteses	parentheses
1457.	finicky	fenecky	finickey	phinicky
1458.	garmient	garmant	garmint	garment
1459.	Haeiti	Haitti	Heati	Haiti
1460.	Wyomerng	Wyomeing	Wyming	Wyoming
1461.	exclusive	exclisive	exclusave	excluseve
1462.	document	documint	docamint	dockument
1463.	Drecule	Draqula	Dracula	Dra-q-la

1464.	lunsh	lonch	lunch	lonsh
1465.	Montrael	Muntreal	Montreal	Montril
1466.	pitch	petch	pitsh	pietch
1467.	Wednisday	Wenesdae	Wednesday	Widnisday
1468.	acroniyms	akronim	acrunyms	acronym
1469.	design	disignt	deesignn	d-sine
1470.	relef	relief	rilieif	relif
1471.	abeviaiton	abbreviation	abbrevietion	abreviation
1472.	period	periodd	piriod	periad
1473.	Muntana	Monteana	Mondtana	Montana
1474.	Virmont	Virmint	Vermount	Vermont
1475.	anonymos	ananymous	anonimous	anonymous
1476.	arithmetic	arithmatic	arithmetick	arethmetic
1477.	August	Augast	Augist	Auguset
1478.	advertesement	advertisement	advertesemet	advertisemint
1479.	chimnee	chemney	chimney	chimnie
1480.	civilization	civelezation	civilication	civilizetion
1481.	taech	teasch	teach	teech
1482.	bicycle	bicyccle	bicecle	bcycle

1483.	brilient	brillient	briliant	brilliant
1484.	definetion	defenetion	definetion	definition
1485.	dangerous	dangirioius	dangeras	dangeros
1486.	feshion	fashion	fashon	fashoin
1487.	fual	phuel	fuel	fuell
1488.	electrracity	electricety	electricity	elecktricity
1489.	cortesy	kortesy	courtesy	coutisy
1490.	exprission	expression	expresion	expresson
1491.	turetle	turtlle	turtle	tartle
1492.	enugh	enoufh	enough	enuff
1493.	closet	claset	clouset	closit
1494.	obtusse	ubtuse	obtoose	obtuse
1495.	canu	caneo	kanoe	canoe
1496.	kanyon	canyon	kaneon	cenyun
1497.	article	articlel	artecle	artickel
1498.	application	appleciation	applicetion	aplication
1499.	cantiidate	candidate	candedate	candydate
1500.	angal	anjel	angel	engel
1501.	angl	angle	ungle	ankel

1502.	amount	amunt	amuont	amont
1503.	forein	foreign	fourgein	foureing
1504.	Freidy	Friday	Frieday	Freday
1505.	founten	fontain	fountain	fountaion
1506.	blizzeard	blezzard	blizzard	blizard
1507.	bargain	bargen	bargaoin	barjain
1508.	reeam	reaem	reem	ream
1509.	gadjet	gadget	gadgit	gadgett
1510.	grocery	grosery	grociery	grocary
1511.	princes	prencess	princiss	princess
1512.	jewearly	jewarly	jewelry	jewarly
1513.	litirature	literature	litereture	laterure
1514.	newclear	nuclar	nuclare	nuclear
1515.	millions	milloins	milion	mellions
1516.	material	materiel	metrial	materoial
1517.	carnivoour	carnivore	canivare	carnivor
1518.	stregight	streigh	straight	striagiht
1519.	apron	aprun	appron	apprun
1520.	pumken	pumken	pumpking	pumpkin

1521.	position	poseshon	pusition	positoin
1522.	graet	greate	great	greaat
1523.	guarantee	guarentee	guerentee	guarentee
1524.	grade	grede	graed	gradde
1525.	grupe	group	guop	gruop
1526.	intellengent	intelligent	entillegent	inteligint
1527.	imposible	imposseble	impossable	impossible
1528.	finishor	finishiur	finisher	finasher
1529.	inoscent	innocent	inocent	innacent
1530.	gymenesum	gymnasium	gynasium	gynesaium
1531.	faithfoll	fathful	faithfull	faithful
1532.	abort	aburt	abourt	abart
1533.	plented	planted	plaunted	plantid
1534.	dreems	draems	drems	dreams
1535.	statemint	statement	stamint	statemont
1536.	preperetion	preparashon	preparation	praparation
1537.	pleasure	plsure	plaesure	pleashure
1538.	priceless	pricceliss	priseles	prycelass
1539.	whellle	whele	wheel	wheal

1540.	tintative	tintetive	teantetive	tentative
1541.	theras	thermas	thermoss	thermos
1542.	microscpae	microscope	mycrosope	microscape
1543.	symphaney	symphony	symphuny	symphonie
1544.	asterisk	asterrick	astirick	asteresk
1545.	polit	pulite	polite	polight
1546.	monolock	monologue	monalogue	monogu
1547.	xhale	exhelle	exhalle	exhale
1548.	dysfunctional	disfunctional	disfunctionel	dysfunckional
1549.	pacifiur	pasifyer	paciefier	pacifier
1550.	pointir	pointer	pointir	pointur
1551.	unconscious	onconscious	uncunscious	unkunscions
1552.	performur	performer	perfourmer	performur
1553.	gamblier	gamblir	gamblur	gambler
1554.	pleayful	plaeyful	playful	pleyfull
1555.	gold	goldd	golld	gollled
1556.	skiing	skieing	skiieng	skinng
1557.	happily	happely	haplily	hapily
1558.	statianery	sationiry	stetionery	stationery

1559.	interrogation	interogetion	interrogashon	interrogetion
1560.	exclemetory	exclamatory	exclametory	exclamatury
1561.	ralative	reletiave	relatife	relative
1562.	Arkanssas	Arkenses	Arckenses	Arkansas
1563.	Nasuaw	Nassau	Nasau	Nassaw
1564.	Jamecia	Jamaeica	Jamaica	Jamaika
1565.	Nicaregua	Nicarague	Nicaragua	Nickaragua
1566.	Guatemaula	Guatemale	Gauatemala	Guatemala
1567.	Columbea	Culumbia	Columbia	Kolumbia
1568.	Equator	Ecuetor	Equetor	Equatur
1569.	Oregun	Uregon	Oregon	Oregan
1570.	Ariezona	Arizune	Arezona	Arizona
1571.	Mississippi	Mississipppe	Missippii	Mississipi
1572.	Brezel	Brazil	Brauzil	Brazal
1573.	Venizuela	Venizuel	Venazuela	Venezuela
1574.	Algerea	Algiria	Algria	Algeria
1575.	Trinidad	Trinedad	Trenedad	Trinaded
1576.	Zambea	Zembia	Zambia	Zambiaia
1577.	Egyppt	Egyttt	Egptt	Egypt

1578.	Ethiopiea	Etheopia	Ethiopia	Etopia
1579.	China	Chena	Chiana	Chaina
1580.	Torkey	Turkey	Turkee	Turkay
1581.	Argintia	Argentina	Argintina	Argentena
1582.	Peru	Perru	Peruu	Peruou
1583.	Belise	Belizze	Belize	Balize
1584.	Japen	Japan	Japin	Jepain
1585.	Madagascar	Madegaescar	Medegasicar	Madacarger
1586.	Amendient	Amendment	Amandment	Amindmint
1587.	stheoscopee	stethescope	stethascop	stethoscope
1588.	telagraph	telegraf	telegraph	talagrahf
1589.	telefhone	telephone	talafone	telephane
1590.	typewriter	typwreter	typewritor	tipewriter
1591.	Oympick	Olympic	Olympick	Oulympc
1592.	pulliey	puley	pulley	polley
1593.	houstage	hustoage	hostege	hostage
1594.	Cairo	Cairow	Cayrow	Caioro
1595.	alleretion	aliteration	allitereshon	alliteration
1596.	mitaphor	matafor	metephor	metaphor

1597.	hyperbole	hyperbowl	hypurbole	hypirbole
1598.	contenent	continent	continant	cuntinent
1599.	cuntrest	contrest	countrast	contrast
1600.	diagram	diegrame	diagrame	diagrum
1601.	doble	doubele	doauble	double
1602.	editir	editur	edator	editor
1603.	essay	essey	esay	essaiy
1604.	expres	express	exprass	exppress
1605.	umbrilla	umbrella	umbrellau	umbrela
1606.	fence	fense	fencce	fencee
1607.	expedete	expidate	expedit	expedite
1608.	Philadalphia	Philedephiai	Philaladalphia	Philadelphia
1609.	Alabamma	Alebama	Alebbama	Alabama
1610.	Jupiter	Jupeter	Jupitur	Jopiter
1611.	Neptune	Neptone	Naptune	Niptune
1612.	Seturn	Saturn	Satirn	Satorn
1613.	Nigeira	Nigira	Negiria	Nigeria
1614.	dicktionary	dictianary	dictionary	dictoinary
1615.	secretary	secratery	secretery	sicretary

1616.	beuty	beauty	baeuty	beaty
1617.	question	queston	questoin	quistion
1618.	textile	textyle	tixtile	textele
1619.	weerd	weirdd	werd	weird
1620.	vegitable	vegetable	vegetabel	vegitable
1621.	usuelly	ussually	uselly	usually
1622.	stilist	styleist	styllist	stylist
1623.	evenntually	eventally	eventually	eventualy
1624.	mentally	meintally	mintally	mentaly
1625.	pastore	pesture	pasture	pashture
1626.	plasure	pleashure	plleasure	pleasure
1627.	pirijudice	pregudice	prejudice	prijudice
1628.	hullk	hulk	holk	hulkk
1629.	Ureneu	Urannus	Uranus	Youranus
1630.	hearse	haerse	hurse	hearce
1631.	demucracy	dimocary	demucracy	democracy
1632.	cactus	cackus	cactous	cacktus
1633.	curbohydrate	carbohydrate	carbuhydrate	carbihydrate
1634.	pezza	pizza	pazza	piza

1635.	tornedo	turnado	tornado	tournado
1636.	journel	journal	jornal	juornal
1637.	smirck	smirrk	smirk	smurk
1638.	golie	goalie	golie	joalie
1639.	cousin	cosin	cousen	coussin
1640.	moscular	musculer	muscular	muskular
1641.	nepew	naphew	nephew	nefew
1642.	neoice	neice	neece	niece
1643.	feather	fether	feathir	faether
1644.	drawer	drawir	drawur	drawor
1645.	neither	neiter	neithor	neithir
1646.	thoug	thog	thouggh	though
1647.	through	throug	thuogh	throough
1648.	bought	baught	boought	buoghht
1649.	braught	brought	brouaght	brauoght
1650.	Hebrrew	Hibrew	Hebrew	Hebreew
1651.	Chenese	Chinnese	Shinese	Chinese
1652.	Portegise	Portugase	Portuguesse	Portuguese
1653.	thousand	thousend	thoasend	thousind

1654.	similar	simeler	similer	similir
1655.	rabiet	rabbet	rabbit	rabbitt
1656.	whele	whale	whalle	whal
1657.	catle	cattel	cuttle	cattle
1658.	langevity	longitivity	longevity	langevity
1659.	gestation	gestestion	gistation	gesstation
1660.	kennel	kenel	kinnel	kennal
1661.	fluid	fluoid	fliud	flewid
1662.	capecity	capesity	capacity	capasity
1663.	mesure	measure	meashure	measare
1664.	centimeter	cintimeter	ceneimeter	centameter
1665.	decameter	decimeter	decimiter	decimater
1666.	additoinel	aditional	additional	addetionel
1667.	entierprise	enterprise	entirprise	enterprase
1668.	astronomy	astronommy	asstronomy	astraunmy
1669.	solar systam	sular system	solir system	solar system
1670.	greviety	gravity	graveity	grevity
1671.	rediation	radiation	radeoitaion	radiaton
1672.	exposure	xposure	expasure	exposhure

1673.	Mercedeis	Mercedes	Mircedis	Mercedas
1674.	Mircury	Mercurry	Mercury	Mercary
1675.	furnature	frrniture	firneture	furniture
1676.	contractir	cuntractor	cantractor	contractor
1677.	Atlanta	Atlandta	Atlenta	Atlantaa
1678.	laminatur	leminator	laminator	laminetur
1679.	menute	minute	minnute	menate
1680.	increese	inckrease	increase	increse
1681.	amount	amunt	amuont	ammount
1682.	miletary	military	militery	militeary
1683.	rotation	routation	rotetion	rotetion
1684.	aproxemate	approximate	approuximate	approximete
1685.	diametir	diemeter	diameter	daimeter
1686.	letitude	latitode	latitude	latetude
1687.	imegene	imagine	imajine	imegine
1688.	Atlentic Oshen	Atlanticd ucean	Atlantiec Ocan	Atlantic Ocean
1689.	Wiscunsin	Wiscansin	Wesconsin	Wisconsin
1690.	firework	farewurk	firrework	fireewark
1691.	Vermont	Virmone	Vermount	Vermant

1692.	Europpe	Earope	Youroupe	Europe
1693.	trageddy	tragedy	treagedy	tregedy
1694.	protagonist	protegonest	protagonest	protagonisst
1695.	flimsy	flimsey	flimssy	flimssey
1696.	conflickt	conflect	conflict	cunflict
1697.	biogreaphy	biogrefy	biography	boigraphy
1698.	symbols	symbel	simbols	symbals
1699.	compere	cumpare	compare	kompare
1700.	diagrem	daigram	diagram	diagramm
1701.	aquereium	aquarioum	aquarium	aquariumm
1702.	minimum	mineumu	minemom	minimam
1703.	percentege	percentage	persentege	percintage
1704.	dunetion	donation	donaetion	doneshon
1705.	Seattel	Seetle	Seatttle	Seattle
1706.	stertle	startle	startel	sturtle
1707.	radiant	redient	radioant	radannt
1708.	thecsaurus	tesaurus	thesaurous	thesaurus
1709.	ligament	ligeamint	ligamint	ligiment
1710.	equiepment	equipment	equipmint	equeipmint

1711.	tidious	tedious	tedias	tedius
1712.	guitar	guitter	geetar	guitir
1713.	amplefer	amplifer	amplipher	amplifier
1714.	scerce	scaerce	scarce	sacarce
1715.	laughtir	laughtur	laughter	laughtor
1716.	edeible	adible	edible	edibele
1717.	octopus	ocktopus	octupos	octoposs
1718.	econamy	economy	econumy	eckonomy
1719.	intierior	ennterior	iinterior	interior
1720.	extirior	xtarior	exterier	exterior
1721.	chronological	chronoloegical	chrenological	kronological
1722.	synchronize	sinchronice	synckhronize	sinchranize
1723.	audable	audeble	audible	audibel
1724.	audetorijm	auditarum	auditorium	audetureum
1725.	centineel	centinneil	cintinnial	centennial
1726.	altirnetive	alternetive	altirnative	alternative
1727.	annually	anually	annally	annuelly
1728.	incision	inceision	incesion	encions
1729.	pricise	pracise	precise	presisse

1730.	incisor	encisor	ncisour	incesor
1731.	coranary	konorary	cunorary	coronary
1732.	adenture	advenshure	adventure	advinture
1733.	incridible	incredeble	incradable	incredible
1734.	dinture	denshure	danture	denture
1735.	dynamight	dynamite	dinamite	dymamaite
1736.	equilebrum	equilibrum	equalibrum	equilibrium
1737.	equinax	equienox	equinax	equinox
1738.	confident	confidant	cunfident	konfident
1739.	flexible	flexable	flexeble	flixible
1740.	tenager	teenegre	teenager	teenger
1741.	dihydrate	dehidrate	dihydraete	dehydrate
1742.	pischology	psycholagy	psychoalogy	psychology
1743.	transcucent	translocent	translucent	transclucint
1744.	manecure	manicure	manecure	menecure
1745.	magnefecent	magnificent	magnifecent	megnecefent
1746.	sinator	senator	seneatir	senetor
1747.	Mediteranean	Mediterranean	Miditerranena	Meditterranen
1748.	memorial	memoreal	memurial	memoreol

1749.	guidence	guydance	gudence	guidance
1750.	prommotion	promoshon	promoution	promotion
1751.	immortal	imortal	immuortal	immortel
1752.	tricycle	triceycle	trycicle	tricyclel
1753.	hazardus	hazerdous	hazardous	hasardous
1754.	knowlidge	knoledge	knowlege	knowledge
1755.	league	leajue	legue	leaguee
1756.	santence	sintence	sentense	sentence
1757.	surplos	sirplus	surrplus	surplus
1758.	tatoo	tatto	tattouo	tattoo
1759.	punishment	punishmint	punishmant	puneshment
1760.	againsst	agenst	ageinst	against
1761.	purmission	pirmission	permision	permission
1762.	vacent	vecant	vakant	vacant
1763.	Bralle	Breille	Braile	Braille
1764.	gasolene	gasuline	gassoline	gasoline
1765.	discrimination	descrimation	discrimation	disrimenation
1766.	boulivard	bolevard	boulevard	bouleverd
1767.	innitial	inetial	initial	initiall

1768.	Nebraska	Niebraska	Nebraks	Nebrauska
1769.	Orogon	Oregon	Origon	Oregun
1770.	Illustrator	Ilustretor	Illostrator	Illustretor
1771.	Australia	Austrelia	Australiea	Austrealia
1772.	pupsicle	popsicle	popsicel	popsycle
1773.	capitaleze	capitalize	capetalize	kapitalize
1774.	holeday	haliday	holliday	holiday
1775.	plurall	plurral	pllural	plural
1776.	nationelity	nationalety	nationality	nashionality
1777.	delacious	deliceous	deliciouss	delicious
1778.	expaession	expresion	exprission	expression
1779.	caterpillar	caterpilar	catirpillar	caturpillar
1780.	coccoon	cocuon	cocon	cocoon
1781.	coufh	caugh	kough	cough
1782.	sandwich	sendwich	sendwhich	sandwish
1783.	violence	violencee	violince	violense
1784.	internat	internet	intirnet	intuernet
1785.	waebsite	webbsite	website	websight
1786.	quotient	qutient	quoshen	quotent

1787.	divdend	dividand	divedend	dividend
1788.	nuclear	nucler	newclear	nucleiar
1789.	marrage	merriage	marriage	mariage
1790.	occasion	ocasion	occesion	occason
1791.	we're'	we're	we'rre	we'r'e
1792.	wouldn't'	wouldn't	wooun't	wouldn't'
1793.	weasn't	wasn't'	wasnn't	wasn't
1794.	shouldn't	schouldn't	shouldn't'	should'n't
1795.	dene't	didnn't	didn't'	didn't
1796.	o'clock	'o'clock	o'clack	o'clocck
1797.	havenn't	haven''t	heaven't	haven't
1798.	soulitary	soletary	solitary	soliteary
1799.	baggage	bagggage	bagage	baggag
1800.	introducktion	intraoduction	intruducton	introduction
1801.	they'll'	they'll	they'l'l	thay'll
1802.	they're	thaey're	they're'	they'ree
1803.	atach	attech	attasch	attach
1804.	corect	currect	correck	correct
1805.	arguoe	arjue	arguee	argue

1806.	pirsuade	persueade	persuade	persuadee
1807.	demonstrate	damonstrate	demunstrate	demonstraite
1808.	paragrafph	paregraph	paragraph	pharagraph
1809.	quote	quot	qouote	quoote
1810.	speech	spaech	spech	spesch
1811.	genetics	jemetic	ganetic	genitics
1812.	quentity	quantity	quentity	qantety
1813.	orthodontist	orthdontist	ortodontist	orthodentist
1814.	hoax	hoaax	haox	hoaxx
1815.	impaty	empathy	ampathy	empethy
1816.	candidete	candidatte	candidate	kanditate
1817.	manecure	menecure	manicure	menicure
1818.	paedicure	pedecure	pedicure	pedikure
1819.	symphony	simpfony	symphany	symfony
1820.	philosophy	philusophy	filosophy	philosaphy
1821.	pindent	pendant	pendent	pendint
1822.	populetion	population	poupulation	pupolation
1823.	manewscript	manoscript	manuscript	manuscrept
1824.	lieghtning	lightening	lighning	lightning

1825.	sausage	sawsage	sauwsage	sausege
1826.	information	informetion	informastion	infourmetion
1827.	outside	outsdice	otside	ouutside
1828.	inspect	inspact	insepct	inspeact
1829.	enspire	enspare	inspere	inspire
1830.	aleignment	aligming	aligment	alignment
1831.	purformence	performence	performance	perfourmance
1832.	survivour	survevor	survevor	survivor
1833.	obiesity	obecity	obeseity	obesity
1834.	measurement	meashurement	mesurement	meshurement
1835.	kaution	caution	caushion	cuation
1836.	plumber	plmaber	plumbir	plubir
1837.	fabulous	fabolous	fabalos	fabolous
1838.	chronolegicel	chronological	cronologiecal	chronulogical
1839.	pamphlet	pamphlit	pamfhlet	pemphlet
1840.	sciniry	sceniry	scenery	seenery
1841.	baemint	basement	basemeant	baysement
1842.	doughnut	dougnot	doughnat	duognit
1843.	geography	goiegraphey	geogrephy	jeography

1844.	geoligst	geologist	geologest	jeologist
1845.	questionnaire	queastionere	questionnere	questannare
1846.	plagaerism	plagarism	plagiarism	plagiaresm
1847.	sororety	surority	sorurity	sorority
1848.	freterniety	fratirnity	fraternity	fraturnity
1849.	procrastinate	procrestenete	procrastenete	pruscrastinate
1850.	risk	resk	rask	risck
1851.	rilesase	releasse	release	relese
1852.	legend	legaend	legind	legand
1853.	Theolegecal	Theological	Theologecal	Theolagical
1854.	ocktagon	octegaon	octagun	octagon
1855.	premare	premiere	premere	premier
1856.	debuete	dabute	debut	dubuut
1857.	alleretion	alleretion	allitteration	alliteration
1858.	turminate	termenete	terminate	terminete
1859.	scorpoin	scarption	scorpon	scorpion
1860.	generation	geneeretion	gineriation	generetion
1861.	Tokeyo	Tuokyo	Tokyou	Tokyo
1862.	urgancy	urgency	urgiency	urgenscy

1863.	Weshinton	Washengton	Washington	Washengton
1864.	jorney	journey	jounay	juorney
1865.	prospirity	prosperity	prospirity	prospereity
1866.	extraordinary	extreordeneary	extraordinatry	extraurdenery
1867.	treashure	treasore	tresure	treasure
1868.	treasurer	tresurer	treashurer	treasurerr
1869.	tresuree	treasury	treasory	treashury
1870.	diverse	dieverse	divurse	deversr
1871.	frantic	frentick	frantick	frentic
1872.	volume	valume	voulume	voluume
1873.	emportent	impurtant	important	impirtant
1874.	cumpromese	comprise	compumese	compromise
1875.	subtence	substence	substance	subtanse
1876.	impeact	impackt	impack	impact
1877.	gelty	guilty	guilety	guelety
1878.	defiendent	defendint	defindant	defendant
1879.	terminel	terminal	turmenel	turminal
1880.	symmetrical	symmetricel	symmetrecal	symetrical
1881.	perticalur	particalir	particular	partikular

1882.	axpertise	expiertise	expertise	expurtice
1883.	pasion	passhon	passion	pession
1884.	contry	countree	kountry	country
1885.	phenomenal	phenmumenal	phunomenal	fenomenal
1886.	demographic	demaographic	demugrafic	demographec
1887.	televesion	television	talavision	televesion
1888.	awdition	audition	audetion	auditshon
1889.	apeal	appeal	appeel	appael
1890.	videow	veideo	videeo	video
1891.	sacrifise	sacrefice	sracrifice	sacrifice
1892.	entertane	enturtain	entirtain	entertain
1893.	swqueeze	squaeeze	squeze	squeeze
1894.	nirvous	narvous	nervous	nurvous
1895.	dolphin	dulphon	dulphin	dofin
1896.	courageous	caourageous	couregoues	koureagou
1897.	vague	vagaue	vegue	vaguee
1898.	cadddie	cadie	caddie	cadei
1899.	lagibly	legebly	legibley	legibly
1900.	greatitude	graitude	gratitode	gratitude

1901.	valentene	valentine	veletine	velentene
1902.	Hallowwen	Haloween	Halloween	Holloween
1903.	purmenent	pirmanent	permenanet	permanent
1904.	halmet	helmit	hellmet	helmet
1905.	realisteic	realistic	realistick	realisitce
1906.	discipline	deiscipline	dicipline	disceipline
1907.	feature	feeature	feasture	feashture
1908.	you're	you're'	yo'u're	you'r'e
1909.	yo'u've	you'v'e	you've	you've'
1910.	they're'	the'y're	they're	they'r'e
1911.	where's'	wher'e's	where's	whe're's
1912.	she'd	she'd'	sh'e'd	she'd'
1913.	have'n't	haven't'	havenn't	haven't
1914.	doens't	doesn't	doesn't'	dosn't
1915.	apostrophe	apoustrouphe	apostrofee	apoustruphe
1916.	akronym	acronyme	acroneem	acronym
1917.	cunstanet	counstant	consunant	consonant
1918.	vaowel	vowell	voweal	vowel
1919.	jeopery	jaeopardy	jeopardey	jeopardy

1920.	spreead	spraed	spread	spreaad
1921.	shadaow	shedown	shadow	shaduw
1922.	pneumania	pneumonia	pneumoneia	neumonoia
1923.	multicultural	multicualral	multeculturel	multicaltural
1924.	prevous	previous	previouus	preveios
1925.	he'll'	he'l'l	he'llll	he'll
1926.	wouldn't'	would'n't	would'nn't	wouldn't
1927.	numerator	numeratur	numaratour	newmerator
1928.	dinomenetor	denominator	denuminetor	denominatur
1929.	hadn't	haddn't	haden't	hadn't'
1930.	isn't	isnn't	is'n't	isnn't'
1931.	leandscape	landskape	lanscape	landscape
1932.	puzzzel	puzzlel	pozzel	puzzle
1933.	architeck	archetick	architack	architect
1934.	excavate	excevete	excevate	xcavate
1935.	meditete	meditate	miditate	meditat
1936.	veloscity	valacity	velocity	velacity
1937.	Nebrasska	Nabraska	Nebreska	Nebraska
1938.	encyclopedia	encyclopedeia	enciclyopedia	encyklopedia

1939.	maillbox	malbox	malebox	mailbox
1940.	progressssively	progresivIly	progressively	progresively
1941.	enginner	engeneer	engineer	enjineer
1942.	aproprete	apropriate	appropriate	apprupriate
1943.	promoshion	promotion	promoshon	promution
1944.	demotion	deemotion	demution	dimoution
1945.	leamorous	glamrous	glamorus	glamorous
1946.	handsome	hendsom	handsum	hansum
1947.	smggy	smuoggy	smogy	smoggy
1948.	filthy	feilthy	filthiy	filhy
1949.	kombative	combative	combeative	combativ
1950.	craawded	crowdied	crowded	crowwded
1951.	braiiny	breainy	brainny	brainy
1952.	therepy	therapy	terabpy	thereppy
1953.	monnopoly	mounopoly	monopoly	monapouly
1954.	campaigne	ceampaign	campagn	campaign
1955.	naughtty	nauhty	noaughty	naughty
1956.	abundant	abbundant	aboundant	abundeant
1957.	comfourtable	comfortable	comortable	comfortabele

1958.	pleasant	pleacsant	pleaseant	pleeasant
1959.	frusstration	frustreation	frustration	frostration
1960.	selfish	selfash	sefash	salfash
1961.	helarious	heilarious	hilarius	hilarious
1962.	fourmula	farmula	furmula	formula
1963.	agreeable	aggreeable	agreeeable	agrable
1964.	morgege	mortgage	mourtgege	mortgege
1965.	audacity	awdacity	audecety	audicity
1966.	internet	intirnat	inturnet	intirnet
1967.	jaundece	jaundice	jauondice	jandece
1968.	remmbrance	remeimbrance	remembrance	rimembrance
1969.	jaersey	gersey	jersey	jirsey
1970.	tolerate	toleraete	tuloreate	tolirate
1971.	plenetarum	planatarum	planetarium	planetareum
1972.	Arezona	Arizona	Arisona	Arizouna
1973.	orchistra	orchestrau	orchestra	orkistra
1974.	voyeage	voyage	vouyage	voyege
1975.	arrengement	arengement	arranjement	arrangement
1976.	facsemelle	facsimile	facsemele	fasimile

1977.	portraie	pourtray	portray	purtrey
1978.	mosquitoes	musquetoes	moskeytoes	mosqutoes
1979.	Europe	Erope	Ewrope	Euroepe
1980.	ignerence	ignoranse	ignorance	ignorence
1981.	Kinya	Kenyaa	Kenyeya	Kenya
1982.	pirspiration	pursperetion	perspiration	purspiration
1983.	pleasant	plesent	pleasent	plesaseant
1984.	muffin	muffen	moffin	mufin
1985.	chemical	chamecal	chemikal	chimecal
1986.	exaistence	existensce	exeistence	existence
1987.	fareword	fourword	fureward	foreword
1988.	herass	hearass	harasss	harass
1989.	indepenseble	indespensible	indispinsible	indispensable
1990.	Maryland	Merylend	Marrylend	Marylaind
1991.	Montene	Muntana	Mutana	Montana
1992.	ryinoceros	rhinocerus	rhinoceros	rinoceross
1993.	catupillars	caterpellars	caterpillars	katerpellars
1994.	woodpeckurs	wodpackers	woodpickers	woodpeckers
1995.	Argintena	Arjentina	Argenena	Argentina

1996.	Brazil	Brazel	Brazeel	Braziel
1997.	Egypt	Eiypt	Eigypt	Egyppt
1998.	Switzurland	Switzirland	Switzerland	Swetzerland
1999.	Vietnam	Vietam	Veitman	Veitnem
2000.	Finland	Fenlend	Finlend	Finnland

ANSWER KEY

1. touch	2. friend	3. paper	4. medicine
5. social	6. deserve	7. bizarre	8. prompt
9. beautiful	10. business	11. secret	12. plastic
13. interest	14. travel	15. tuition	16. terrific
17. academy	18. ready	19. gorgeous	20. happier
21. played	22. push	23. international	24. decision
25. mention	26. acceptance	27. recognition	28. familiar
29. calendar	30. graduation	31. accusation	32. meaningful
33. perfect	34. because	35. vacation	36. sensible
37. publication	38. fortunate	39. adaptation	40. happiness
41. reciprocate	42. chemical	43. recently	44. finally
45. elaborate	46. nursery	47. changeable	48. cherish
49. harmless	50. further	51. collaboration	52. relationship
53. address	54. decision	55. separation	56. unlimited
57. dependable	58. certainly	59. reality	60. independent
61. difference	62. popular	63. emotion	64. significant
65. proportion	66. dedicated	67. university	68. desperate
69. identify	70. between	71. fluid	72. conclusive
73. dramatically	74. conclusion	75. technique	76. relax
77. hamster	78. company	79. introduction	80. highway
81. tension	82. chinese	83. reflection	84. responsibility
85. continuation	86. sweater	87. heater	88. temperature
89. provoke	90. frustration	91. continue	92. almanac
93. circumstance	94. estimate	95. demanded	96. genetic
97. addicted	98. appliance	99. recognition	100. puncture
101. straight	102. development	103. enrollment	104. dramatic
105. elimination	106. height	107. mountain	108. envelope
109. laundry	110. leather	111. jacket	112. cheese
113. discount	114. detergent	115. produce	116. gallon
117. quality	118. itinerary	119. encyclopedia	120. problem
121. sophistication	122. claim	123. remorse	124. defendant
125. neighbor	126. brought	127. argument	128. scooter
129. refrigerator	130. intervene	131. intermission	132. tomorrow
133. magnificent	134. fascinated	135. politics	136. socially
137. profession	138. language	139. essential	140. notice
141. estimate	142. economy	143. dumbbell	144. security
145. supplier	146. trouble	147. sure	148. rough

149. criminal	150. school	151. financial	152. rescue
153. federal	154. industry	155. executive	156. recession
157. though	158. spiral	159. support	160. minimize
161. choreographer	162. commercial	163. exclusive	164. document
165. original	166. restaurant	167. confuse	168. transfer
169. around	170. connection	171. excited	172. impress
173. allowance	174. realize	175. humor	176. awful
177. classified	178. estimate	179. responsible	180. designer
181. appointment	182. emergency	183. liquidation	184. computer
185. digital	186. anxious	187. immediately	188. century
189. special	190. fantastic	191. majestic	192. collection
193. personality	194. comfortable	195. direction	196. famous
197. leisure	198. critic	199. decade	200. national
201. expert	202. represent	203. weird	204. definition
205. ridiculous	206. satisfaction	207. situation	208. multipurpose
209. imagination	210. hospital	211. automobile	212. American
213. spelling	214. opportunity	215. activity	216. energy
217. exercise	218. inspired	219. hurricane	220. beard
221. numeric	222. features	223. numerous	224. process
225. payment	226. transition	227. receipt	228. diamond
229. children	230. storage	231. luxury	232. furniture
233. union	234. Hollywood	235. grocery	236. bottle
237. valley	238. avenue	239 climate	240. pioneer
241. lemonade	242. national	243. pledge	244. problem
245. sensational	246. carnation	247. daisies	248. jungle
249. background	250. summary	251. summarize	252. daffodil
253. iris	254. marigold	255. orchid	256. tulip
257. surgery	258. disturb	259. arrogant	260. annoy
261. combative	262. confuse	263. condemn	264. massive
265. miniature	266. immense	267. Germany	268. France
269. Mexico	270. England	271. China	272. Doberman
273. Poodle	274. Boxer	275. Rottweiler	276. Collie
277. valuable	278. intermediate	279. settler	280. equality
281. noticeable	282. offender	283. Pilgrim	284. explorer
285. scarcity	286. Thanksgiving	287. landform	288. season
289. timeline	290. river	291. peninsula	292. minister
293. parade	294. freedom	295. standard	296. courage
297. download	298. backward	299. inspired	300. hospital

301. grammar	302. vocabulary	303. scream	304. translation
305. diskettes	306. dynamite	307. inheritance	308. attachment
309. answer	310. presence	311. mountains	312. enemy
313. tribulation	314. Russia	315. generosity	316. imitation
317. vegetables	318. convince	319. exercise	320. measure
321. uniform	322. strength	323. against	324. heritage
325. continue	326. citizen	327. rocket	328. peace
329. textile	330. employer	331. transfer	332. Utah
333. temporary	334. tough	335. reaction	336. precious
337. defense	338. acquainted	339. knowledge	340. apology
341. scrutinize	342. detective	343. vacation	344. terminal
345. anticipate	346. factory	347. together	348. gentlemen
349. location	350. victory	351. fruit	352. employment
353. headache	354. signature	355. guarantee	356. monster
357. wealth	358. group	359. dollar	360. visible
361. forbidden	362. emit	363. devastated	364. daughter
365. facility	366. ability	367. incredible	368. famous
369. destruction	370. function	371. blizzard	372. Philadelphia
373. Georgia	374. permit	375. convertible	376. California
377. basically	378. peculiar	379. purchase	380. strange
381. surround	382. beauty	383. promotion	384. scissor
385. million	386. Commissioner	387. lightning	388. confusion
389. establish	390. Connecticut	391. investigation	392. apartment
393. identify	394. energy	395. narrate	396. narrative
397. narrator	398. pertain	399. prudent	400. multitude
401. calamity	402. transgression	403. separates	404. reveal
405. subscription	406. instruction	407. persuade	408. continue
409. proportion	410. property	411. emotion	412. ordinary
413. respect	414. jewelry	415. warranty	416. country
417. photograph	418. viewer	419. suddenly	420. charity
421. dissolve	422. astonishment	423. creature	424. fugitive
425. manufacture	426. appropriate	427. authority	428. continually
429. consideration	430. compare	431. warehouse	432. station
433. contemplate	434. discuss	435. lobster	436. effort
437. air	438. attorney	439. numerator	440. millionaire
441. science	442. dancer	443. wisdom	444. half
445. dangerous	446. evening	447. preposition	448. character
449. presenter	450. denominator	451. fourth	452. third

453. compromise	454. horoscope	455. horizontal	456. several
457. reconciliation	458. necessity	459. roommate	460. income
461. expense	462. increase	463. labor	464. resource
465. should	466. hopefully	467. further	468. official
469. civilian	470. earthquake	471. patient	472. Cherokee
473. garage	474. inauguration	475. triplet	476. refusal
477. procrastinate	478. compassion	479. traffic	480. problem
481. meteorologist	482. ahead	483. billboard	484. toothbrush
485. seafood	486. insurance	487. urgent	488. bridge
489. amount	490. depend	491. kitchen	492. cleaner
493. customer	494. transmission	495. permission	496. freedom
497. therapy	498. reduction	499. community	500. corner
501. husband	502. theater	503. shoulder	504. whether
505. material	506. available	507. conversation	508. example
509. Christmas	510. decoration	511. expensive	512. natural
513. formula	514. transcript	515. league	516. leadership
517. magazine	518. standard	519. across	520. navigate
521. plastic	522. literally	523. freezer	524. consumer
525. productive	526. therapist	527. greater	528. counselor
529. realtor	530. amusement	531. veterinary	532. optician
533. company	534. pharmacy	535. health	536. message
537. restraint	538. harvest	539. partner	540. annual
541. percentage	542. equity	543. divide	544. multiply
545. fraction	546. luminous	547. kitten	548. conductor
549. factory	550. warning	551. warehouse	552. afternoon
553. around	554. trumpet	555. frantic	556. kindergarten
557. animals	558. review	559. birthday	560. government
561. literacy	562. dangerous	563. enough	564. geometry
565. middle	566. another	567. basement	568. upstairs
569. picnic	570. castle	571. accident	572. laugh
573. mattress	574. carpet	575. reason	576. tremble
577. orchard	578. heavy	579. morning	580. nature
581. already	582. again	583. surprise	584. piece
585. written	586. unbutton	587. porch	588. elevator
589. escalate	590. approach	591. official	592. leader
593. effective	594. journal	595. application	596. February
597. collection	598. Wednesday	599. academy	600. Thursday
601. several	602. symbol	603. piano	604. curtain

605. compromise	606. genius	607. weekly	608. difference
609. sentence	610. citation	611. equally	612. literature
613. responsible	614. legible	615. oven	616. naturally
617. battle	618. milkshake	619. enterprise	620. gorilla
621. giraffe	622. quality	623. rhinoceros	624. Africa
625. scientist	626. politics	627. nutritionist	628. barrel
629. identify	630. supermarket	631. transmission	632. hygiene
633. Georgia	634. advancement	635. particular	636. umbrella
637. wholesale	638. aggression	639. achievement	640. fundamentally
641. accountable	642. breakfast	643. hostage	644. pumpkin
645. commercial	646. expedite	647. trillions	648. massage
649. celebrate	650. accomplish	651. expansion	652. visionary
653. global	654. common	655. commitment	656. president
657. family	658. announce	659. announcement	660. pronunciation
661. articulate	662. secondary	663. environmental	664. democratic
665. auction	666. Massachusetts	667. addition	668. bulletin
669. sanitizer	670. original	671. crystal	672. geographic
673. national	674. deliver	675. underline	676. wireless
677. protection	678. confidence	679. circumstances	680. world
681. earth	682. cooperation	683. substitute	684. attitude
685. pageant	686. certification	687. crypt	688. employment
689. annual	690. combination	691. foreign	692. companion
693. abundant	694. resource	695. almanac	696. weather
697. decision	698. stadium	699. constitution	700. nationality
701. guarantee	702. direction	703. watermelon	704. February
705. pressure	706. dictation	707. speculation	708. litigation
709. section	710. liquidation	711. experience	712. delight
713. Australian	714. embarrassed	715. specific	716. journal
717. baboon	718. appreciation	719. sensitive	720. musical
721. entertainment	722. research	723. pertain	724. selective
725. hibernate	726. shampoo	727. powerful	728. marriage
729. rehearsal	730. Louisiana	731. Antarctica	732. Hemisphere
733. Equator	734. Argentina	735. remnant	736. connection
737. internet	738. consignment	739. impression	740. hamburger
741. Connecticut	742. addition	743. birthday	744. sleeveless
745. practice	746. greatest	747. Geographic	748. interpretation
749. simplify	750. underline	751. strength	752. protection
753. confidence	754. circumstances	755. house	756. homograph

757. spelling	758. shepherd	759. attitude	760. miserable
761. readable	762. kangaroo	763. coyotes	764. mammal
765. January	766. purple	767. December	768. resolution
769. confetti	770. costume	771. keyboard	772. television
773. graphic	774. fantastic	775. dramatic	776. accelerate
777. cabbage	778. recognize	779. alteration	780. minimize
781. representation	782. traditional	783. Virginia	784. wonderful
785. reduction	786. practical	787. administration	788. enhancement
789. campaign	790. investigation	791. gesture	792. solicitation
793. Tallahassee	794. Mississippi	795. prioritize	796. perpendicular
797. examination	798. critical	799. government	800. cycle
801. transfer	802. bankrupt	803. collapse	804. stampede
805. gorilla	806. scripture	807. candidate	808. speech
809. ballerina	810. regulation	811. residence	812. defrost
813. picture	814. signature	815. ceramic	816. install
817. complicate	818. grapefruit	819. kiwi	820. improvement
821. irresponsible	822. debate	823. educator	824. chaos
825. appearance	826. fingernail	827. eyebrow	828. Canadian
829. alternator	830. routine	831. coverage	832. payment
833. transparency	834. children	835. Illinois	836. recommend
837. physician	838. technician	839. anniversary	840. Afghanistan
841. ferret	842. Pennsylvania	843. electric	844. stadium
845. apron	846. retailer	847. electrician	848. reporter
849. intelligent	850. veteran	851. prosecutor	852. Alaska
853. demolish	854. accusation	855. treatment	856. priority
857. charity	858. potato	859. headlight	860. program
861. volcano	862. explode	863. magnificent	864. kilogram
865. destructive	866. productive	867. cautiously	868. easily
869. accident	870. pronounce	871. purpose	872. research
873. commune	874. ostrich	875. searching	876. hummingbird
877. underground	878. perfume	879. invalid	880. future
881. discharge	882. insert	883. entrance	884. demonstration
885. shield	886. fountain	887. classic	888. science
889. Washington	890. maintain	891. persuade	892. persuasion
893. completion	894. definition	895. transform	896. support
897. evaluate	898. character	899. publisher	900. suspension
901. museum	902. skateboard	903. offense	904. humiliation
905. resentment	906. proficient	907. hyper	908. explain

909. fruit	910. banana	911. soccer	912. daffodil
913. behavior	914. yesterday	915. musician	916. submarine
917. quantity	918. minute	919. respect	920. plumber
921. oven	922. toaster	923. microwave	924. blender
925. cylinder	926. lavender	927. violet	928. rhinestone
929. granulated	930. daisy	931. height	932. ignorance
933. immediate	934. humorous	935. jewelry	936. judgment
937. library	938. license	939. millennium	940. miniature
941. maintenance	942. principal	943. questionnaire	944. referred
945. reference	946. rhyme	947. schedule	948. vacuum
949. souvenir	950. pamphlets	951. particular	952. opinion
953. occasionally	954. permanent	955. syllable	956. tendency
957. flour	958. specifically	959. symmetrical	960. strategy
961. sincerely	962. withdrawal	963. outrageous	964. prescription
965. struggle	966. championship	967. business	968. hypocrite
969. courtesy	970. character	971. characteristic	972. criticize
973. information	974. interrupt	975. island	976. exaggerate
977. enemy	978. beneficial	979. companion	980. desperate
981. appearance	982. accommodate	983. amateur	984. address
985. magazine	986. reaction	987. clarification	988. laboratory
989. lieutenant	990. controversial	991. September	992. perjury
993. ordinary	994. decrease	995. anniversary	996. peaceful
997. appropriate	998. property	999. suggest	1000. office
1001. former	1002. author	1003. governor	1004. familiar
1005. bizarre	1006. surreal	1007. realize	1008. corner
1009. option	1010. impeachment	1011. conference	1012. credibility
1013. politically	1014. situation	1015. accuse	1016. marvelous
1017. force	1018. article	1019. opinion	1020. effective
1021. railroad	1022. interest	1023. require	1024. election
1025. selection	1026. capable	1027. because	1028. syllable
1029. memorial	1030. extended	1031. seasonal	1032. Halloween
1033. English	1034. emotional	1035. dealership	1036. sympathy
1037. sheriff	1038. privacy	1039. security	1040. wealthy
1041. condominium	1042. condition	1043. concrete	1044. conclusion
1045. sense	1046. servant	1047. condition	1048. thrilled
1049. aroma	1050. arrogant	1051. eighteen	1052. purchase
1053. provoke	1054. magnet	1055. machinery	1056. institution
1057. intelligent	1058. installment	1059. infection	1060. influence

1061. moderate	1062. question	1063. raspberry	1064. qualification
1065. puzzle	1066. swamp	1067. syrup	1068. syringe
1069. purse	1070. varieties	1071. expense	1072. expire
1073. interview	1074. excuse	1075. advance	1076. accomplish
1077. supportive	1078. creative	1079. enjoy	1080. community
1081. luggage	1082. grease	1083. occurrence	1084. misspell
1085. personnel	1086. argument	1087. illiterate	1088. absolutely
1089. statistical	1090. inclement	1091. postcard	1092. believe
1093. discipline	1094. column	1095. collectible	1096. category
1097. recital	1098. rebuild	1099. equipment	1100. experience
1101. ancestor	1102. selective	1103. similar	1104. Mexico
1105. Colorado	1106. Utah	1107. Rhode Island	1108. Europe
1109. France	1110. transform	1111. establishment	1112. orchestra
1113. aspiration	1114. expression	1115. energy	1116. Michigan
1117. Detroit	1118. efficiency	1119. convince	1120. failure
1121. hundred	1122. simultaneously	1123. engage	1124. approach
1125. determine	1126. question	1127. purpose	1128. outline
1129. vigilant	1130. command	1131. dangerous	1132. anticipate
1133. potential	1134. copycat	1135. intelligence	1136. effective
1137. pressure	1138. primary	1139. security	1140. progress
1141. Arkansas	1142. Minnesota	1143. deadline	1144. distract
1145. compromise	1146. fragrance	1147. important	1148. campaign
1149. Brazil	1150. Venezuela	1151. incomplete	1152. inspire
1153. trigger	1154. detachable	1155. forehead	1156. measure
1157. describe	1158. challenge	1159. manager	1160. stapler
1161. sure	1162. rush	1163. whales	1164. vanilla
1165. strawberry	1166. flavor	1167. stranger	1168. reaction
1169. humiliate	1170. exhausted	1171. congratulations	1172. rebound
1173. malnutrition	1174. married	1175. psychologist	1176. optometrist
1177. fleece	1178. dentist	1179. dietitian	1180. country
1181. sympathy	1182. removable	1183. January	1184. shaken
1185. cruise	1186. beautician	1187. triathlon	1188. original
1189. jeopardy	1190. academic	1191. vital	1192. headache
1193. esophagus	1194. masterpiece	1195. flamboyant	1196. fabric
1197. passion	1198. image	1199. instrument	1200. wardrobe
1201. retriever	1202. Collie	1203. Borzoi	1204. Spaniel
1205. appreciate	1206. retirement	1207. vampire	1208. sweater
1209. polyester	1210. radiant	1211. circulate	1212. clever

1213. sheepdog	1214. buffalo	1215. beaver	1216. badger
1217. antelope	1218. camel	1219. buzzard	1220. penguin
1221. parrot	1222. hyena	1223. porcupine	1224. weasel
1225. mayor	1226. tarantula	1227. zip code	1228. company
1229. gymnasium	1230. deduction	1231. ocean	1232. nourishment
1233. nutrition	1234. illuminate	1235. enclose	1236. karaoke
1237. shoulder	1238. traded	1239. propose	1240. advise
1241. qualified	1242. agreement	1243. wrong	1244. premises
1245. evacuate	1246. solution	1247. private	1248. kangaroo
1249. elevator	1250. escalator	1251. elevate	1252. appointment
1253. dentistry	1254. from	1255. when	1256. which
1257. each	1258. know	1259. water	1260. calculator
1261. second	1262. stallion	1263. example	1264. toward
1265. himself	1266. necklace	1267. surface	1268. voice
1269. escape	1270. rehabilitation	1271. identification	1272. connection
1273. amazing	1274. trampoline	1275. distinction	1276. couple
1277. handsome	1278. novelty	1279. memorable	1280. navigate
1281. cholesterol	1282. chicken	1283. package	1284. damage
1285. deodorant	1286. leadership	1287. donation	1288. juice
1289. international	1290. early	1291. ketchup	1292. Paris
1293. banner	1294. season	1295. instrument	1296. champion
1297. depict	1298. patron	1299. tomatoes	1300. ingredient
1301. shield	1302. Equator	1303. presenter	1304. identify
1305. extremely	1306. opinion	1307. unique	1308. postpone
1309. applicant	1310. reminder	1311. economy	1312. accessible
1313. average	1314. consignment	1315. allergic	1316. arthritis
1317. fierce	1318. maneuver	1319. suspicious	1320. detective
1321. exquisite	1322. revision	1323. consequence	1324. disinfected
1325. ballistic	1326. eligible	1327. intrigued	1328. invasion
1329. defiant	1330. hideous	1331. discrimination	1332. therapeutic
1333. resume	1334. transplant	1335. transient	1336. vindictive
1337. peaches	1338. experience	1339. conclusion	1340. deliberately
1341. interrupting	1342. mysterious	1343. snatching	1344. extension
1345. Milwaukee	1346. obnoxious	1347. conviction	1348. canopy
1349. slavery	1350. believe	1351. money	1352. penny
1353. quarter	1354. nickel	1355. insurance	1356. arson
1357. bogus	1358. suffocate	1359. succumb	1360. similarities
1361. polynomial	1362. diminutive	1363. anonymous	1364. fluorescent

1365. microfilm	1366. eccentric	1367. volume	1368. debris
1369. charitable	1370. perimeter	1371. vibrate	1372. nuggets
1373. produce	1374. alimony	1375. residue	1376. porcelain
1377. camouflage	1378. canter	1379. coincidence	1380. skeptical
1381. predator	1382. fierce	1383. gratitude	1384. negotiate
1385. conflict	1386. indicator	1387. scripture	1388. prosperity
1389. marsupial	1390. ancestor	1391. generation	1392. renovate
1393. stabilize	1394. partial	1395. aggressive	1396. damage
1397. colony	1398. worst	1399. parade	1400. potential
1401. carousel	1402. exercise	1403. alphabet	1404. cooperative
1405. lotion	1406. peanut	1407. delivery	1408. empty
1409. mirror	1410. building	1411. envelope	1412. instant
1413. sinister	1414. pastry	1415. chocolate	1416. ticket
1417. squirrel	1418. prison	1419. newsstand	1420. score
1421. newspaper	1422. learn	1423. parent	1424. biography
1425. compare	1426. explain	1427. narrative	1428. descriptive
1429. describe	1430. tennis	1431. glance	1432. poach
1433. punctuation	1434. riddle	1435. polite	1436. disastrous
1437. insect	1438. Texas	1439. chain	1440. president
1441. dimple	1442. surgery	1443. doctor	1444. dignitary
1445. struggle	1446. exaggeration	1447. humor	1448. language
1449. siren	1450. technology	1451. customer	1452. morning
1453. California	1454. dialogue	1455. apostrophe	1456. parentheses
1457. finicky	1458. garment	1459. Haiti	1460. Wyoming
1461. exclusive	1462. document	1463. Dracula	1464. lunch
1465. Montreal	1466. pitch	1467. Wednesday	1468. acronym
1469. design	1470. relief	1471. abbreviation	1472. period
1473. Montana	1474. Vermont	1475. anonymous	1476. arithmetic
1477. August	1478. advertisement	1479. chimney	1480. civilization
1481. teach	1482. bicycle	1483. brilliant	1484. definition
1485. dangerous	1486. fashion	1487. fuel	1488. electricity
1489. courtesy	1490. expression	1491. turtle	1492. enough
1493. closet	1494. obtuse	1495. canoe	1496. canyon
1497. article	1498. application	1499. candidate	1500. angel
1501. angle	1502. amount	1503. foreign	1504. Friday
1505. fountain	1506. blizzard	1507. bargain	1508. ream
1509. gadget	1510. grocery	1511. princess	1512. jewelry
1513. literature	1514. nuclear	1515. millions	1516. material

1517. carnivore	1518. straight	1519. apron	1520. pumpkin
1521. position	1522. great	1523. guarantee	1524. grade
1525. group	1526. intelligent	1527. impossible	1528. finisher
1529. innocent	1530. gymnasium	1531. faithful	1532. abort
1533. planted	1534. dreams	1535. statement	1536. preparation
1537. pleasure	1538. priceless	1539. wheel	1540. tentative
1541. thermos	1542. microscope	1543. symphony	1544. asterisk
1545. polite	1546. monologue	1547. exhale	1548. dysfunctional
1549. pacifier	1550. pointer	1551. unconscious	1552. performer
1553. gambler	1554. playful	1555. gold	1556. skiing
1557. happily	1558. stationery	1559. interrogation	1560. exclamatory
1561. relative	1562. Arkansas	1563. Nassau	1564. Jamaica
1565. Nicaragua	1566. Guatemala	1567. Columbia	1568. Equator
1569. Oregon	1570. Arizona	1571. Mississippi	1572. Brazil
1573. Venezuela	1574. Algeria	1575. Trinidad	1576. Zambia
1577. Egypt	1578. Ethiopia	1579. China	1580. Turkey
1581. Argentina	1582. Peru	1583. Belize	1584. Japan
1585. Madagascar	1586. Amendment	1587. stethoscope	1588. telegraph
1589. telephone	1590. typewriter	1591. Olympic	1592. pulley
1593. hostage	1594. Cairo	1595. alliteration	1596. metaphor
1597. hyperbole	1598. continent	1599. contrast	1600. diagram
1601. double	1602. editor	1603. essay	1604. express
1605. umbrella	1606. fence	1607. expedite	1608. Philadelphia
1609. Alabama	1610. Jupiter	1611. Neptune	1612. Saturn
1613. Nigeria	1614. dictionary	1615. secretary	1616. beauty
1617. question	1618. textile	1619. weird	1620. vegetable
1621. usually	1622. stylist	1623. eventually	1624. mentally
1625. pasture	1626. pleasure	1627. prejudice	1628. hulk
1629. Uranus	1630. hearse	1631. democracy	1632. cactus
1633. carbohydrate	1634. pizza	1635. tornado	1636. journal
1637. smirk	1638. goalie	1639. cousin	1640. muscular
1641. nephew	1642. niece	1643. feather	1644. drawer
1645. neither	1646. though	1647. through	1648. bought
1649. brought	1650. Hebrew	1651. Chinese	1652. Portuguese
1653. thousand	1654. similar	1655. rabbit	1656. whale
1657. cattle	1658. longevity	1659. gestation	1660. kennel
1661. fluid	1662. capacity	1663. measure	1664. centimeter
1665. decimeter	1666. additional	1667. enterprise	1668. astronomy

1669. solar system	1670. gravity	1671. radiation	1672. exposure
1673. Mercedes	1674. Mercury	1675. furniture	1676. contractor
1677. Atlanta	1678. laminator	1679. minute	1680. increase
1681. amount	1682. military	1683. rotation	1684. approximate
1685. diameter	1686. latitude	1687. imagine	1688. Atlantic Ocean
1689. Wisconsin	1690. firework	1691. Vermont	1692. Europe
1693. tragedy	1694. protagonist	1695. flimsy	1696. conflict
1697. biography	1698. symbols	1699. compare	1700. diagram
1701. aquarium	1702. minimum	1703. percentage	1704. donation
1705. Seattle	1706. startle	1707. radiant	1708. thesaurus
1709. ligament	1710. equipment	1711. tedious	1712. guitar
1713. amplifier	1714. scarce	1715. laughter	1716. edible
1717. octopus	1718. economy	1719. interior	1720. exterior
1721. chronological	1722. synchronize	1723. audible	1724. auditorium
1725. centennial	1726. alternative	1727. annually	1728. incision
1729. precise	1730. incisor	1731. coronary	1732. adventure
1733. incredible	1734. denture	1735. dynamite	1736. equilibrium
1737. equinox	1738. confident	1739. flexible	1740. teenager
1741. dehydrate	1742. psychology	1743. translucent	1744. manicure
1745. magnificent	1746. senator	1747. Mediterranean	1748. memorial
1749. guidance	1750. promotion	1751. immortal	1752. tricycle
1753. hazardous	1754. knowledge	1755. league	1756. sentence
1757. surplus	1758. tattoo	1759. punishment	1760. against
1761. permission	1762. vacant	1763. Braille	1764. gasoline
1765. discrimination	1766. boulevard	1767. initial	1768. Nebraska
1769. Oregon	1770. Illustrator	1771. Australia	1772. popsicle
1773. capitalize	1774. holiday	1775. plural	1776. nationality
1777. delicious	1778. expression	1779. caterpillar	1780. cocoon
1781. cough	1782. sandwich	1783. violence	1784. internet
1785. website	1786. quotient	1787. dividend	1788. nuclear
1789. marriage	1790. occasion	1791. we're	1792. wouldn't
1793. wasn't	1794. shouldn't	1795. didn't	1796. o'clock
1797. haven't	1798. solitary	1799. baggage	1800. introduction
1801. they'll	1802. they're	1803. attach	1804. correct
1805. argue	1806. persuade	1807. demonstrate	1808. paragraph
1809. quote	1810. speech	1811. genetics	1812. quantity
1813. orthodontist	1814. hoax	1815. empathy	1816. candidate
1817. manicure	1818. pedicure	1819. symphony	1820. philosophy

1821. pendant	1822. population	1823. manuscript	1824. lightning
1825. sausage	1826. information	1827. outside	1828. inspect
1829. inspire	1830. alignment	1831. performance	1832. survivor
1833. obesity	1834. measurement	1835. caution	1836. plumber
1837. fabulous	1838. chronological	1839. pamphlet	1840. scenery
1841. basement	1842. doughnut	1843. geography	1844. geologist
1845. questionnaire	1846. plagiarism	1847. sorority	1848. fraternity
1849. procrastinate	1850. risk	1851. release	1852. legend
1853. Theological	1854. octagon	1855. premiere	1856. debut
1857. alliteration	1858. terminate	1859. scorpion	1860. generation
1861. Tokyo	1862. urgency	1863. Washington	1864. journey
1865. prosperity	1866. extraordinary	1867. treasure	1868. treasurer
1869. treasury	1870. diverse	1871. frantic	1872. volume
1873. important	1874. compromise	1875. substance	1876. impact
1877. guilty	1878. defendant	1879. terminal	1880. symmetrical
1881. particular	1882. expertise	1883. passion	1884. country
1885. phenomenal	1886. demographic	1887. television	1888. audition
1889. appeal	1890. video	1891. sacrifice	1892. entertain
1893. squeeze	1894. nervous	1895. dolphin	1896. courageous
1897. vague	1898. caddie	1899. legibly	1900. gratitude
1901. valentine	1902. Halloween	1903. permanent	1904. helmet
1905. realistic	1906. discipline	1907. feature	1908. you're
1909. you've	1910. they're	1911. where's	1912. she'd
1913. haven't	1914. doesn't	1915. apostrophe	1916. acronym
1917. consonant	1918. vowel	1919. jeopardy	1920. spread
1921. shadow	1922. pneumonia	1923. multicultural	1924. previous
1925. he'll	1926. wouldn't	1927. numerator	1928. denominator
1929. hadn't	1930. isn't	1931. landscape	1932. puzzle
1933. architect	1934. excavate	1935. meditate	1936. velocity
1937. Nebraska	1938. encyclopedia	1939. mailbox	1940. progressively
1941. engineer	1942. appropriate	1943. promotion	1944. demotion
1945. glamorous	1946. handsome	1947. smoggy	1948. filthy
1949. combative	1950. crowded	1951. brainy	1952. therapy
1953. monopoly	1954. campaign	1955. naughty	1956. abundant
1957. comfortable	1958. pleasant	1959. frustration	1960. selfish
1961. hilarious	1962. formula	1963. agreeable	1964. mortgage
1965. audacity	1966. internet	1967. jaundice	1968. remembrance
1969. jersey	1970. tolerate	1971. planetarium	1972. Arizona

1973. orchestra	1974. voyage	1975. arrangement	1976. facsimile
1977. portray	1978. mosquitoes	1979. Europe	1980. ignorance
1981. Kenya	1982. perspiration	1983. pleasant	1984. muffin
1985. chemical	1986. existence	1987. foreword	1988. harass
1989. indispensable	1990. Maryland	1991. Montana	1992. rhinoceros
1993. caterpillars	1994. woodpeckers	1995. Argentina	1996. Brazil
1997. Egypt	1998. Switzerland	1999. Vietnam	2000. Finland

There are ten misspelled words in these stories. Circle the misspelled words.

Cristina's Birthday Party

Whaen Cristina turned tin, her mom and dad had a birthday party for her. Thirty of her closest freinds came to her party. Everyone wore birthday hats and had birthday cake. The birthday cake was colored pink and white, which are Cristina's favoriete colors.

As the day went on, the cheldrin played keckkbaul and hide and seek in the backyard. Cristina pleayed third base, Andrew played outfield, and Cristina's dad was the pitchur.

At the end of the party, Cristina asked her parents if she could have next yeers birthday at the skating rink. Her parents agreed and evereewon jumped and cheered.

July Is The Hottest Month

I woke up one Jully morneng in a warm sweat. I ran to the freezur to get a cold drink, but it was bruken and all the drinks were as hot as the sun. I turned on my elictrack fan, but it wasn't wurking either. I quickly turned on the telivision and realized that the electrecety in my house was completly out.

Later that afternoon, I went to the neighborhood pool with my friend Jeremy to cool off. The temperature was 100 degrees. My friend Jeremy bought me an ice cream sendwech from the ice cream truck. Even though the weather was extremely hot, I enjoyed myself at the pool.

Andrew Hurt His Elbow

Andrew was going to the pleaygrund with his best freind Brian. On his way to the playground, he tripped and screaped his elbow. Andrew penecked and started screaming for his mom. Luckily Andrew's mom heard his screaming and came running. Andrew's mom came pripared with a first aid kit. She got a wet towel, a bandeage, and two strauburry ice cream sendweiches. Soon Andrew was on his wey pleying with his friend Brian.

Jenny Likes To Run

Jenny likes to run. Ever since she was in fourth grade she has been treneng to run long destences. Now that she is in the ninth grade, her parents agreed to let her run in the Hawaiian Classic. The Hawaiian Classic is a ten kelomiter run. It takes place every year in Hawaii. The wenner gets a lifetime supply of mixed fruits and fruit juices from Melanie's Juice Store.

Jenny practiced by running every morning four times a week. On the avareje run, she wuld finish in twenty five minutes and ten seconds.

On the day of the race, Jenny ran faster than she ever had in the past. As she came ackruss the last kilometer she was in third place. She picked up the pace and quickly into second place, just as she cud see the finish line. She ran to the fenesh line, but she just wasn't fast enuf to get ahead of Tiffany.

ANSWER KEY
CRISTINA'S BIRTHDAY PARTY

1. When
2. ten
3. friends
4. favorite
5. children
6. kickball
7. played
8. pitcher
9. years
10. everyone

ANSWER KEY
JULY IS THE HOTTEST MONTH

1. July
2. morning
3. freezer
4. broken
5. electric
6. working
7. television
8. electricity
9. completely
10. sandwich

ANSWER KEY
ANDREW HURT HIS ELBOW

1. playground
2. friend
3. scraped
4. panicked
5. prepared
6. bandage
7. strawberry
8. sandwiches
9. way
10. playing

ANSWER KEY
JENNY LIKES TO RUN

1. training
2. distances
3. kilometer
4. winner
5. average
6. would
7. across
8. could
9. finish
10. enough

Matching

Misspelled	Correct Spelling
1. Baloon	Perfect
2. Caushon	Gymnasium
3. Pracktece	Delicious
4. Chickin	Salad
5. Purfact	Kitchen
6. Penceke	People
7. Jeckit	Grasshopper
8. Ketchin	Caution
9. Malemain	Baseball
10. Dennur	World
11. Hondread	Mouth
12. Seled	Chicken
13. Wiating	Balloon
14. Bassebaul	Practice
15. Poepel	Hundred
16. Muoth	Popcorn
17. Dilicouis	Dinner
18. Gresshuper	Pancake
19. Wurdl	Waiting
20. Lawnn	Mailman
21. Gimnasium	Lawn
22. Pupcurn	Jacket

MATCHING
ANSWER KEY

1.   Balloon
2.   Caution
3.   Practice
4.   Chicken
5.   Perfect
6.   Pancake
7.   Jacket
8.   Kitchen
9.   Mailman
10.   Dinner
11.   Hundred
12.   Salad
13.   Waiting
14.   Baseball
15.   People
16.   Mouth
17.   Delicious
18.   Grasshopper
19.   World
20.   Lawn
21.   Gymnasium
22.   Popcorn

VOCABULARY WORDS SHEET

1._____

2._____

3._____

4._____

5._____

6._____

7._____

8._____

9._____

10._____

11._____

12._____

13._____

14._____

15._____

16._____

17._____

18._____

19._____

20._____

CREATE YOUR OWN SENTENCES SHEET

1._____

2._____

3._____

4._____

5._____

6._____

7._____

8._____

9._____

10._____

11._____

12._____

13._____

14._____

15._____

16._____

17._____

18._____

19._____

20._____

ABOUT THE AUTHOR

In order to know how to write effectively, students must know how to spell words correctly. Being an educator for over 8 years and observing students writing and spelling, I have learned that it takes time and patience to teach students how to become successful spellers.

In recent years, I've had the urge to help children with their spelling skills. I felt writing this book might serve that purpose. In preparing to do so, I read quite a few books on How to Help Children Learn to Spell.

Like many books on any given subject, some have been very stimulating and helpful and others less so, at least in connection to the purpose of this book. Unlike other books on the subject, my book provides a thoughtful, easy-to-read strategies for students to become successful spellers.

Such as,

1.   Writing the same words four times and use the word in a sentence
2.   Playing fun spelling games
3.   Using Flashcards
4.   Covering the word and saying it in their mind
5.   Read books, newspapers, magazines that contains many new words
6.   Create a spelling dictionary
7.   Learn to proofread your writing

I also tutor elementary students in several subjects and I emphasize the importance of spelling correctly.

I feel excited to be involved in a career that allows me to help students succeed in their academic goals.